*Maya Angelou's*

# I Know Why the Caged Bird Sings

*Text by*
**Anita Davis**
*(Ed.D., Duke University)*
Department of Education
Converse College
Spartanburg, South Carolina

*Illustrations by*
**Karen Pica**

***Research & Education Association***

*MAXnotes*™ for
I KNOW WHY THE CAGED BIRD SINGS

Copyright © 1994 by Research & Education Association. All rights reserved. No part of this book may be reproduced in any form without permission of the publisher.

Printed in the United States of America

Library of Congress Catalog Card Number 94-65963

International Standard Book Number 0-87891-956-2

*MAXnotes*™ is a trademark of
Research & Education Association, Piscataway, New Jersey 08854

# *What* **MAXnotes**™ *Will Do for You*

This book is intended to help you absorb the essential contents and features of Maya Angelou's *I Know Why the Caged Bird Sings* and to help you gain a thorough understanding of the work. The book has been designed to do this more quickly and effectively than any other study guide.

For best results, this **MAXnotes** book should be used as a companion to the actual work, not instead of it. The interaction between the two will greatly benefit you.

To help you in your studies, this book presents the most up-to-date interpretations of every section of the actual work, followed by questions and fully explained answers that will enable you to analyze the material critically. The questions also will help you to test your understanding of the work and will prepare you for discussions and exams.

Meaningful illustrations are included to further enhance your understanding and enjoyment of the literary work. The illustrations are designed to place you into the mood and spirit of the work's settings.

The **MAXnotes** also include summaries, character lists, explanations of plot, and chapter-by-chapter analyses. A biography of the author and discussion of the work's historical context will help you put this literary piece into the proper perspective of what is taking place.

The use of this study guide will save you the hours of preparation time that would ordinarily be required to arrive at a complete grasp of this work of literature. You will be well-prepared for classroom discussions, homework, and exams. The guidelines that are included for writing papers and reports on various topics will prepare you for any added work which may be assigned.

The **MAXnotes** will take your grades "to the max."

Dr. Max Fogiel
Program Director

# Contents



**Each chapter includes List of Characters, Summary, Analysis, Study Questions and Answers, and Suggested Essay Topics.**

# SECTION ONE

# *Introduction*

***The Life and Work of Maya Angelou***

Maya Angelou, named Marguerite Johnson at birth, is the daughter of Vivian Baxter Johnson and Bailey Johnson, a doorman and naval dietitian. Angelou was born on April 4, 1928, in St. Louis, Missouri. She had one brother, Bailey.

As children, Bailey and Marguerite moved from St. Louis to Long Beach, California, to Stamps, Arkansas, to St. Louis and back to Stamps. After her eighth-grade graduation, Marguerite moved to San Francisco to live with her mother.

Marguerite became the first Black female ticket collector on the streetcars in San Francisco. She graduated from high school in California. At 16 she had her son there. The birth of her illegitimate son concludes *I Know Why the Caged Bird Sings.* Angelou states in *Current Biography* (1974) that this happy event is the best thing that ever happened to her.

Maya Angelou's life has been an eventful one. She served in 1960–61 as Northern coordinator for the Reverend Dr. Martin Luther King's Southern Christian Leadership Conference and as a key aide to Malcolm X. She worked in Africa as associate editor of a Cairo English newsweekly and for the *Ghanian Times* and as a Pan-African soldier. Angelou acted in the TV series *Roots* and has written 10 books; she has received more than 30 honorary doctorates. She directed and wrote the script and music for the screen version of *I Know Why the Caged Bird Sings.* Angelou served under

President Jimmy Carter as a member of the National Commission on the Observance of International Women's Year, under President Gerald Ford on the American Revolution Bicentennial Advisory Council, and as a poet/participant at the inauguration of President Bill Clinton. In London the National Society for the Prevention of Cruelty to Children named its new facility the Maya Angelou Child Protection Team and Family Center.

Maya Angelou admits that she has done many things, but she sees herself first as a "Black American female writer." (*Essence*, May 1992) The imposing, six-foot tall woman often works sixteen-hours a day when she is writing. Her talent has also been recognized by Wake Forest University in North Carolina, where she is Reynolds Professor.

### *Historical Background*

The autobiographical *I Know Why the Caged Bird Sings* spans a period of time from 1931 until 1944. The realistic portrayal of Angelou's life is set against the Depression and World War II. Her homes, the Store, and the church which figured prominently into her life are described in great detail. Her depiction of the socially and racially divided cities and towns of St. Louis, Stamps, and California help the reader to understand life in America—from the viewpoint of a "Southern Black girl"—during this time period. Because of her firsthand knowledge of life during this time and because of her honesty in recording the settings and the events in her life, reviewers have said that she has used "the clay of real life" in her writings. (*Essence*, May 1992)

### *Master List of Characters*

**Marguerite Johnson**—*The narrator and main character, she is three-years-old when the story begins and about sixteen when the story ends.*

**Bailey Johnson, Jr.**—*The brother of Marguerite, he is a year older than his sister.*

**Mrs. Annie Henderson**—*The grandmother of Marguerite and Bailey, she lives in Stamps.*

**Uncle Willie Johnson**—*Marguerite's crippled uncle, Uncle Willie*

*Johnson is the brother of Bailey Johnson, Jr., and the person for whom Wm. Johnson General Merchandise Store is named.*

**Mr. Steward**—*A former sheriff, Mr. Steward pays the family a visit to tell "Willie he better lay low tonight."*

**Mr. McElroy**—*Mr. McElroy lives next to the Store and sells patent medicine.*

**Reverend Howard Thomas**—*Reverend Thomas presides over a district that includes Stamps.*

**Sister Monroe**—*Sister Monroe is a church member who often "gets the spirit" and shouts during the service.*

**Reverend Taylor**—*Reverend Taylor is the pastor of the church Marguerite attends.*

**Deacon Jackson**—*A deacon, Mr. Jackson becomes involved in an emotional church scene with Sister Monroe.*

**Sister Willson**—*Sister Willson is chair of the usher board.*

**Mr. Murphy**—*The third husband of Mrs. Annie Henderson, Mr. Murphy comes to visit once while Marguerite is there.*

**Mr. Johnson**—*Mrs. Henderson's first husband, Mr. Johnson is Marguerite's grandfather.*

**Bailey Johnson, Sr.**—*Bailey is Mrs. Annie Henderson's son and Marguerite's father.*

**Vivian Baxter Johnson**—*Marguerite's mother is Mother Dear to Bailey and Bibbi to friends.*

**Powhitetrash**—*Marguerite uses the word "Powhitetrash" to refer to the dirty, ill-mannered white people who live on Mrs. Henderson's land and treat Mrs. Henderson, Uncle Willie, and Marguerite very rudely.*

**The Baxter Family**—*Vivian's family consists of Grandmother Baxter and Vivian's brothers (particularly Tutti, Ira, and Tom) and lives in St. Louis at first.*

**Mr. Freeman**—*Mr. Freeman is the live-in friend of Vivian, the children's mother.*

**Pat Patterson**—*Pat Patterson offends Vivian and suffers the consequences.*

**Mrs. Bertha Flowers**—*Mrs. Flowers brings Marguerite to her Stamps home to visit and sets an example for her.*

**Viola Cullinan**—*Marguerite's employer, Mrs. Cullinan treats Marguerite with contempt and will not even call Marguerite by her proper name.*

**Miss Glory**—*Miss Glory is the longtime employee of Mrs. Cullinan.*

**Kay Francis**—*Miss Francis is the movie star who looks like Vivian Baxter.*

**Brother Bishop, Miss Duncan** and **Miss Grace**—*These are the flat characters who attend the tent revival.*

**Joe Louis**—*Louis is the Brown Bomber, a champion boxer during the 1930s.*

**Louise Kendricks**—*Louise is Marguerite's best friend.*

**Tommy Valdon**—*Tommy is the first "sweetheart" of Marguerite.*

**Miss Williams**—*Miss Williams is Marguerite's seventh-grade teacher.*

**Joyce**—*Joyce is Bailey's first sexual encounter.*

**Mrs. Goodman**—*Mrs. Goodman is a customer in the Store.*

**Mr. George Taylor**—*Mr. Taylor is a widower who visits and chills Marguerite with tales.*

**Miss Kirwin**—*Miss Kirwin is a California educator who influences Marguerite.*

**Daddy Clidell**—*Clidell is Mother's friend who is kind to Marguerite.*

**Boarders and Underworld Characters** (including **Red Leg, Black**)—*These flat characters are a part of life in Daddy Clidell's home.*

**Dolores Stockland**—*Dolores, the mistress of Marguerite's father, knifes Marguerite.*

**Lee Arthur and Bootsie**—*These are two of the junkyard friends.*

**Marguerite's Son and the Child's Father**—*These characters are nameless.*

***Summary of the Novel***

*I Know Why the Caged Bird Sings* is the autobiography of Marguerite Johnson, later known as Maya Angelou. The book takes the reader from Marguerite's arrival in Stamps, Arkansas, to the birth of her son.

Through the writer's vivid portrayals of events, the reader experiences Marguerite's insecurity, her love of family, her church and school experiences which were so important in her growing up, and her visits to her mother and father. On one of these visits to her mother's, Marguerite is raped by her mother's friend. The ultimate result of this violation is his death at the hands of Mother Dear's brothers. Marguerite is mute for some time after this. (Some sources say she did not speak for five years.)

Marguerite describes in detail how she returns to Stamps and is at last able to make two friends: Mrs. Flowers and Louise Kendricks. As Marguerite matures she is able to observe the social order around her in Stamps. She describes the church picnic, the congregating of the neighbors in the Store to hear the fights on the radio, and the pride of the community in the eighth-grade graduation exercises. All the while, the young narrator is observing the class and caste system of the South.

It is after her brother encounters a man being dragged from the river that her grandmother takes her to California to live with her mother. Marguerite is impressed with how her grandmother, who has never before left the vicinity of Stamps, is able to function in a new social structure. Marguerite makes the reader aware of the class and caste system which exists in the West. It is when her father invites her to visit him in another town in California that she becomes aware of still another social structure.

Her father lives with Dolores Stockland, who becomes very angry when Marguerite goes with her father into Mexico and does not return until the next day. An argument ensues and Dolores cuts Marguerite. Marguerite's father is ashamed and embarrassed by the incident and leaves Marguerite with friends; Marguerite runs away.

Marguerite spends her first night in a junkyard and wakes the next morning to find faces peering in the windows at her. She meets a gang of juveniles who live in the junked cars and who have their own code of conduct. Marguerite makes her home with them for a month and finds her insecurity dislodged. She at last calls her mother for plane fare home.

Marguerite breaks racial barriers in California when she secures employment as the first Black employee on the San Francisco streetcars. Even though she has found security with the junkyard gang, Marguerite has trouble dealing with her own sexuality and wonders if she is developing normally. After reading a book on lesbianism, she fears that she is lesbian. To satisfy her questions and to find out about her "normalcy" once and for all, Marguerite decides to have sex and try to work out a relationship with one of two brothers who live near her home. Three weeks later, with her questions still unanswered, Marguerite finds herself pregnant.

Marguerite keeps her secret from everyone but Bailey and manages to graduate from high school about three weeks before the birth of her son. The book ends with Marguerite accepting the care and support of the child she loves.

The most important theme in *I Know Why the Caged Bird Sings* is the maturation of Marguerite and, to a lesser degree, the growth and development of Bailey. Both these characters are growing, changing, *dynamic* characters, in contrast to Mrs. Annie Henderson, their stable, caring grandmother who is a *static* character.

### *Estimated Reading Time*

The average silent reading rate for a secondary student is 250 to 300 words per minute. Since each page has about 400 words on it, an average student would take about 2 minutes to read each page. The total reading time for the 246-page book would be about 8 hours. Reading the book according to the natural chapter breaks is the best approach.

# SECTION TWO

# *I Know Why the Caged Bird Sings*

## Preface

New Character:

**Marguerite:** *the narrator, a "Southern Black girl"*

***Summary***

Marguerite remembers an Easter service which is painful for her to recall. Her day is a terrible one from the time she puts on her "cut-down" Easter dress. During the Easter program Marguerite forgets her lines, trips on her way out of the church, and wets her pants. Marguerite escapes to her home with her wet clothes even though she knows she will be spanked for leaving the service. Still, she manages to feel joy because she is liberated from the service and because she feels a physical release from the pressure on her bladder.

***Analysis***

Readers encounter many conflicts in the Preface which captivate their interest. A first conflict is character-against-society when Marguerite explains her dissatisfaction with her life. She dreams of wearing a beautiful dress and looking "like one of the sweet little white girls." She longs to hear people saying, "'forgive us, please, we didn't know who you were."' She imagines waking one day and finding her hair is long and blond. She decides that a wicked fairy has turned her into a "too-big Negro girl, with nappy black hair, broad feet and a space between her teeth that would hold a number-two pencil."

A character-against-nature conflict occurs when Marguerite attempts to control her bladder during the service. She says, however, that "a green persimmon, or it could have been a lemon, caught me between the legs and squeezed . . . Then before I reached the door, the sting was burning down my legs and into my Sunday socks."

The reader is also aware of a third conflict: character-against-character. Marguerite says she is going to get a whipping for running home—but she laughs anyway. One's interest is captured and we are eager to find out more about the home life of this unhappy child.

Stylistic devices abound in *I Know Why the Caged Bird Sings.* For instance, Angelou uses *hyperbole* when Marguerite describes her urge to urinate; Marguerite says that it felt as if "my poor head would burst like a dropped watermelon, and all the brains and spit and tongue and eyes would roll all over the place." She uses *connotation* when she describes her dress length as "old-lady long" and *similes* when she says her skin is "dirty like mud" when she longs to look "like a movie star." *Imagery* is used to describe the Easter dress on that fateful day:

> The dress I wore was lavender taffeta, and each time I breathed it rustled, and now that I was sucking in air to breathe out shame it sounded like crepe paper on the back of hearses.

The dominant theme of the autobiographical *I Know Why the Caged Bird Sings* is that of the growth and maturation of the author. One sees the narrator at an immature time in her life; she is not able to control bodily functions or present her part in the Easter program. We know, however, that the young character will grow. Angelou concludes the Preface by saying:

> If growing up is painful for the Southern Black girl, being aware of her displacement

is the rust on the razor that threatens
the throat.
It is an unnecessary insult.

***Study Questions***

1. What leads you to believe the events described in the Preface are painful to recall?
2. At what church was the narrator performing?
3. What color was the narrator's Easter dress?
4. How had the narrator kept her legs soft?
5. What was the line she forgot?
6. How did the children react to the narrator's forgetting her line?
7. How did Marguerite further humiliate herself?
8. Why did the narrator believe she would be whipped?
9. Who tried to help Marguerite when she forgot her lines?
10. Why was Marguerite laughing even though she knew that she would get a whipping?

***Answers***

1. The narrator says that she had not so much forgotten as she had not been able to bring herself to remember.
2. The narrator was performing at the Colored Methodist Episcopal Church.
3. She had a lavender taffeta dress.
4. She kept her skin soft by greasing it with Blue Seal Vaseline.
5. The line was, "I just come to tell you it's Easter Day."
6. The children laughed at her for forgetting.
7. Marguerite humiliated herself by wetting her pants.
8. The narrator believed she would be whipped for leaving church.

9. The preacher's wife tried to help Marguerite when she forgot her lines.
10. Marguerite was able to laugh because of the joy of leaving the church and from the knowledge that her head would not burst from the build-up of urine.

***Suggested Essay Topics***

1. The narrator describes herself at various points in the Preface. Give a written description of the narrator. Do you think the narrator has a positive self-image? Explain.
2. The narrator fantasizes during the Preface. What are some of her fantasies?

# Chapter 1

New Characters:

**Bailey Johnson, Jr.:** *Marguerite's four-year-old brother*

**Mrs. Annie Henderson:** *Marguerite's grandmother and a resident of Stamps, Arkansas*

***Summary***

Chapter 1 tells of the arrival of Marguerite and Bailey at their grandmother's after their parents' divorce. Marguerite describes in detail the setting of Stamps, Arkansas, and specifically the Wm. Johnson General Merchandise Store. Through her eyes the reader sees the activities in the Store each day.

***Analysis***

Since Marguerite is only three-years-old when the story begins, the reader knows that the narrator is remembering the events of an earlier time. Marguerite is a *round character,* one which is revealed in entirety to the reader—the reader knows all about Marguerite. Her thoughts, feelings, and reactions are all evident since Marguerite tells everything to her audience.

Angelou uses *personification,* or giving human characteristics to inanimate objects. For example, she tells us that "the town reacted to us as its inhabitants had reacted to all things new before our coming." She uses *connotation*—a reference to something else—when she says that the field was "caterpillar green." She uses a *simile* in "it [the town] closed in around us, as a real mother embraces a stranger's child."

The *dialect* is typical of Southerners during the Depression era.

For example, one of the customers says, "Lemme have a hunk uh cheese and some sody crackers." The plot of the novel is *progressive,* since the reader has to read the whole story to reach the climax—the highest point of interest, and the denouement—the ending.

*Imagery* is used to describe the Store and the workers. The reader is aware of sights, sounds, feelings, and smells as Marguerite describes what she finds in the Store in the morning and at night. In the morning the Store is filled with "laughing, joking, boasting, and bragging" workers. The tired field workers would "fold down, dirt-disappointed, to the ground" at the end of the day. "The people dragged, rather than their empty cotton sacks. No matter how much they had picked, it wasn't enough."

The rigid caste system of the South during the Great Depression is an important part of the realism of *I Know Why the Caged Bird Sings.* In Chapter 1 the narrator describes the hopelessness of the system's victims—the cotton-pickers:

> . . . In cotton-picking time the late afternoons
> revealed the harshness of Black Southern
> life, which in the early morning had been
> softened by nature's blessing of grogginess,
> forgetfulness and the soft lamplight.

***Study Questions***

1. What town is the setting for *I Know Why the Caged Bird Sings*?
2. How old was the narrator when she arrived by train?
3. What are the names of the two children in the chapter?
4. Why were they going to Arkansas?
5. What was the name and relation of the woman who would care for them?
6. How did the cotton-pickers described by Marguerite differ from the cotton-pickers depicted in movies and other media?
7. How did Uncle Willie make his living?
8. What was the name of the Store in Chapter 1?

9. Why did the cotton pickers stop by the store in the mornings?
10. What time did the owner of the store rise during picking season?

***Answers***

1. The town of Stamps, Arkansas, is the setting for *I Know Why the Caged Bird Sings.*
2. The narrator was three years old when she arrived by train.
3. The two children in the chapter are Marguerite and Bailey Johnson, Jr.
4. The children were going to Arkansas since their parents had separated; they would stay with a relative there.
5. The grandmother who would care for them was Mrs. Annie Henderson.
6. In the media the cotton-pickers were depicted as laughing and singing; Marguerite, on the other hand, had seen their tiredness, their cuts, and their hopelessness.
7. Mrs. Annie Henderson and Uncle Willie ran a general store.
8. The name of the store was Wm. Johnson General Merchandise Store.
9. The cotton-pickers stopped at the store in the morning to pick up food for their lunch and to be picked up to go to the fields.
10. The owner of the Store got up at 4:00 in the morning.

***Suggested Essay Topics***

1. The setting is an important part of *I Know Why the Caged Bird Sings.* Describe the Store in the morning. What smells, sights, etc. are there? Contrast this with a store opening in this day and time.
2. Contrast the pickers in the morning and in the evening.

# Chapter 2

New Character:

**Uncle Willie:** *the son of Mrs. Annie Anderson and the uncle of Marguerite and Bailey.*

### *Summary*

In Chapter 2 Marguerite describes Uncle Willie in detail and also shares with the reader her "first white love"—William Shakespeare. Marguerite also tells how Uncle Willie listens to the children recite and threatens them against the cherry-red stove if they miss a fact.

### *Analysis*

Characterization is a prominent feature in Chapter 2, as Marguerite describes Uncle Willie in detail. "Uncle Willie used to sit, like a giant black Z (he had been crippled as a child) . . . " Despite this, Uncle Willie pretends to himself and to others that he is not in fact lame.

Marguerite reveals much about the caste and class system in Stamps when she describes the way that Uncle Willie is approached by "our society, where two-legged, two-armed strong Black men" treat "Uncle Willie, with his starched shirts, shined shoes and shelves full of food" as "the whipping boy and butt of jokes of the underemployed and underpaid."

In Chapter 2, the children have already grown and matured from Chapter 1. Bailey is now six and Marguerite is five. The children have not just grown older; they have grown in their skills and abilities and their understanding of society.

### *Study Questions*

1. What handicap did Uncle Willie have?
2. Who was Uncle Willie's mother?
3. Why did his mother say he was handicapped?
4. How did Uncle Willie punish the children if they made a second mistake on their times tables?

5. Who was Marguerite's first white "love"?
6. How did Marguerite pacify herself about Shakespeare's whiteness?
7. Who was the poet that Marguerite and Bailey memorized?
8. What was the name of the poem that they memorized?
9. Why did Marguerite deliberately jump toward the stove?
10. Why was Marguerite not burned when she jumped toward the stove?

### *Answers*

1. Uncle Willie was crippled; he also had a secondary handicap because he stuttered.
2. Uncle Willie's mother was Annie Henderson.
3. Annie Henderson said that Willie was handicapped because a babysitter dropped him on his head.
4. Uncle Willie would push the children toward the dull red heater if their faltered on their times tables.
5. Marguerite's first white "love" was William Shakespeare.
6. She pacified herself about his whiteness by "saying that after all he had been dead so long it couldn't matter to anyone any more."
7. The children memorized the poet James Weldon Johnson.
8. The poem they memorized was "The Creation."
9. Marguerite deliberately lunged toward the stove to remove "the possibility of its remaining a threat." She thought that if she could "face the worst danger voluntarily, and triumph, [she] would forever have power over it."
10. Marguerite was not burned because Uncle Willie held tight to her dress.

### *Suggested Essay Topics*

1. Describe Uncle Willie's teaching methods. How do his meth-

ods differ from those of a typical elementary school teacher? How are they the same?

2. Angelou uses a young child to reveal Uncle Willie to the reader. What does she tell the reader about Uncle Willie? Describe the tragedy of Willie's lameness as told through Marguerite. Can a young, innocent narrator present an accurate picture of Uncle Willie? Explain your answer.

# Chapter 3

New Character:

**Mr. Steward:** *the former sheriff*

### *Summary*

In Chapter 3 Marguerite reveals her pleasure in working in the Store, always written with a capital *S.* Marguerite also describes the visit of Mr. Steward, the past sheriff of Stamps, to warn Uncle Willie to "lay low tonight." Mr. Steward explains that some of the "boys" will be visiting because "a crazy nigger messed with a white lady today." Marguerite tells how they conceal Uncle Willie in the vegetable bins in the Store and how he moans all through the night.

### *Analysis*

Conflicts are an important part of Chapter 3. Character-against-society conflict is apparent with the visit from Mr. Steward to tell Uncle Willie to hide from the Klan. The tense racial situation in Depression-era Stamps is evident when Marguerite describes how Uncle Willie and "every other Black man . . . would scurry under their houses to hide in chicken droppings" when the Klan rode.

A conflict also occurs between Mr. Steward and Marguerite. Marguerite remarks that she "would be unable to say anything in his behalf." She again makes the reader aware of the caste and class system in the rural South and the volatile emotions associated with the system.

Another conflict is one that Marguerite imposes upon herself in the Store. She tries to measure the flour, mash, meal, sugar, or corn exactly right the first time she puts it on the scale. If she makes an error with the first try, she "would quietly but persistently punish herself. For every bad judgment, the fine was no silver-wrapped Kisses."

*I Know Why the Caged Bird Sings* continues to be a maturational novel. Marguerite no longer merely observes the happenings in the Store; she readily participates in the activities. Her insights into the happenings of the Klan are those of a much more mature child than the one who first arrived in Stamps.

Mr. Steward is portrayed to the reader through Marguerite's eyes. The narrator's portrayal of Mr. Steward is enhanced through the use of imagery: "The used-to-be sheriff sat rakishly astraddle his horse. His nonchalance was meant to convey his authority and power." Angelou uses personification in referring to the Store; she says, "I sensed that it was tired. I alone could hear the slow pulse of its job half done." Angelou uses a simile to describe the Store in the mornings; she writes that "it looked like an unopened present from a stranger." A metaphor is employed to describe opening the front doors in the statement that opening the door "was pulling the ribbon off the unexpected gift." In the phrase "thudding the ground" onomatopoeia is used.

***Study Questions***

1. How did Marguerite punish herself for inaccuracy in measurement?
2. Marguerite seems obsessed with a certain food. Which food is it?
3. Why did Marguerite not open a can of this food and eat it?
4. What was supper in the Store?
5. What was the dirtiest of chores that Marguerite and Bailey performed?
6. What had been the occupation of Mr. Steward?
7. Who were "the boys" that Mr. Steward referred to when he came?

8. Where did the family hide Uncle Willie after Mr. Steward's visit?
9. Why would Uncle Willie have been found if "the boys" had come?
10. Where was Marguerite's favorite place to be?

***Answers***

1. Marguerite punished herself by not eating a chocolate kiss.
2. Marguerite is obsessed with pineapple.
3. Marguerite would not open a can because the smell would remain on her hands and her actions would be discovered.
4. Supper in the Store was crackers, onions, and sardines.
5. Marguerite and Bailey's dirtiest chore was feeding the pigs.
6. Mr. Steward was once a sheriff.
7. "The boys" were actually the Ku Klux Klan.
8. Uncle Willie was hidden in the vegetable bins in the Store.
9. Uncle Willie would have been found because he moaned all night.
10. Marguerite's favorite place to be was the Store.

***Suggested Essay Topics***

1. Marguerite performed many tasks about the Store and home. Why would Marguerite consider feeding the pigs one of the worst of the chores? Do you think that Marguerite during the Depression had to assume more responsibilities than children today? Explain your answer.
2. Mr. Steward came to tell the family to hide Uncle Willie. Why was Marguerite angry at Mr. Steward about this? Describe hiding Uncle Willie. What was Uncle Willie's reaction to the hiding? Why do you think that Uncle Willie behaved in this manner?

# Chapter 4

New Character:

**Mr. McElroy:** *lives in the big rambling house next to the Store*

### *Summary*

Marguerite presents a portrait of Mr. McElroy, who lives next to the Store and sells patent medicines. She also discusses her relationship with Bailey, who was the greatest person in the world and her protector when adults said unkind things to her. Marguerite depicts two customs of Stamps: canning and curing, and the delicious meals from the smokehouse, the shelves, and the garden. An important part of the chapter is the description of segregation in Stamps; in fact, the segregation is so complete that in the 1930s "most Black children didn't really, absolutely know what whites looked like." Marguerite recalls that she "couldn't force myself to think of them [whites] as people . . . People were those who lived on my side of town."

### *Analysis*

In Chapter 4, Bailey pits himself against those who speak unkindly to Marguerite. For example, when Mrs. Coleman, or anyone, comments upon the features of Marguerite, Bailey immediately comes to her defense. Bailey, in an oily voice, insults Mrs. Coleman—or whoever heaps impolite comments upon Marguerite—by asking if her son is better; when Mrs. Coleman asks what he is sick from, Bailey would answer with a straight face, "From the Uglies."

Marguerite must control her laughter at Bailey's antics. She finds it necessary to "hold my laugh, bite my tongue, grit my teeth and very seriously erase even the touch of a smile from my face." Marguerite often has a difficult time controlling herself, an indication that she is still a child at this point in the novel.

Marguerite cannot force herself to think of whitefolks as people. She explains that "People were those who lived on my side of town. I didn't like them all, or, in fact, any of them very much, but they were people. These others . . . weren't considered folks.

They were whitefolks." She discusses the "hostility of the powerless against the powerful, the poor against the rich, the worker against the worked for, and the ragged against the well dressed." In Stamps the segregation is complete and the feelings the separation produces are depicted carefully by Angelou.

The autobiographical *I Know Why the Caged Bird Sings* is a maturational novel. One can sense the change in size and maturity of Marguerite since Chapter 2. In fact she tells us that much of this story is told "from the perch of age."

***Study Questions***

1. Whom did Marguerite consider "people"?
2. Why could whitefolks not be "people"?
3. Why did the people who did laundry pull items from the baskets to show others?
4. What meat did Mrs. Henderson buy twice a year?
5. Why did whites have fresh meat often?
6. Where did Marguerite and Bailey get meat the rest of the year?
7. What foods were preserved in Stamps?
8. Why did the men take a round bone from the ham knuckle?
9. Why was Bailey not punished often?
10. What need does every lonely child have?

***Answers***

1. Marguerite considered people to be those who lived on her side of town.
2. "Whitefolks couldn't be people because their feet were too small, their skin too white and see-throughy, and they didn't walk on the balls of their feet . . . they walked on their heels like horses."
3. The people would take out a piece to show their talent for ironing or to show the fine things owned by their employers.

4. Mrs. Henderson bought liver twice a year.
5. Whites had meat often because they had refrigeration.
6. Bailey and Marguerite had meat from their smokehouse most of the year.
7. In Stamps anything that could be preserved was canned.
8. It "could make the meat go bad."
9. Bailey was not punished often because he was the pride of the Henderson/Johnson family.
10. Every lonely child has "the unshaking need for an unshakable God."

***Suggested Essay Topics***

1. Marguerite and Bailey have the same parents and are growing up together. What similarities do you see between the two characters? What are the contrasts that you see?
2. Marguerite presents the reader with a look at the segregated Stamps of the 1930s. Describe Stamps as it was when Marguerite was growing up there. What differences would you expect to find there more than half a century later?

# Chapter 5

New Characters:

**Powhitetrash:** *poor, dirty, ill-mannered white children who live on Mrs. Henderson's land and antagonize her*

### *Summary*

Mrs. Henderson demands cleanliness and manners from her grandchildren. These habits are foreign to the powhitetrash who live on Mrs. Henderson's land. On the afternoon in question, Marguerite has just completed sweeping the yard and has made a design in the dirt. Mrs. Henderson looks admiringly at the design and sees the powhitetrash approaching. Mrs. Henderson sends Marguerite inside and faces the children alone. They laugh at her and imitate her, and then one of the girls stands on her head and reveals that she has no underpants. Through it all Mrs. Henderson sings hymns. As they leave, she says goodbye to each girl by name; Marguerite describes her grandmother's face as shining as she looks at her. Marguerite sweeps the yard again and this time makes designs of concentric hearts with a piercing arrow.

### *Analysis*

Chapter 5 is fraught with conflict as the powhitetrash children directly confront Mrs. Henderson. The children mock her and taunt her. For instance, when one tries to imitate her, another says, "Naw, you can't do it. Your mouth ain't pooched out enough." The children do not recognize Mrs. Henderson as a human being because of her color, an expression of the caste system in rural Stamps.

Mrs. Henderson refuses to become agitated when the powhitetrash, one segment of Stamps society, mock her personally. She faces the white society by singing and never losing her composure. Marguerite sees the strength in her grandmother who faces the system but does not bend or break.

Angelou uses many stylistic devices in this chapter to help the reader visualize the confrontation between Mrs. Henderson and the powhitetrash. Imagery helps the reader see the children clearly: "Their greasy uncolored hair hung down, uncombed, with a grim

Wm. Johnson

finality." Marguerite's narration tells the story effectively: "one of them wrapped her right arm in the crook of her left." Marguerite continues to be a round character—the reader knows all about Marguerite's thoughts, feelings, and reactions. For instance, Marguerite tells us, "I thought about the rifle behind the door, but I knew I'd never be able to hold it straight."

The reader sees firsthand the clash of those in different castes in the setting of rural Stamps, Arkansas. The reader also sees the triumph of Mrs. Henderson as she acts and refuses to react to those who mock her. In this way, social realism is an important part of the chapter.

Angelou lightens the harshness of the chapter by showing another side of Mrs. Henderson: a sense of humor. This is evident when Mrs. Henderson would instruct Marguerite to "wash as far as possible, then wash possible."

***Study Questions***

1. What were the two commandments of Mrs. Henderson?
2. What was the joke Grandmother Henderson told as she instructed the children to bathe carefully?
3. Why was Marguerite afraid to draw water at night?
4. Where must one never look to show respect?
5. What term was given to the dirty white children who had no manners?
6. What did Marguerite do to make the yard outside the Store more attractive?
7. What design did Marguerite make before the children came?
8. What design did Marguerite make after the children came?
9. What did Mrs. Henderson do while the children mocked her?
10. How did Mrs. Henderson feel after the children left?

***Answers***

1. "Thou shall not be dirty" and "Thou shall not be impudent" were Grandmother Henderson's two commandments.

2. Grandma Henderson told the children to "wash as far as possible, then wash possible."
3. Marguerite was afraid to draw water at night because she was afraid snakes might come.
4. One must never look in a person's face if one wishes to show respect.
5. Marguerite called the dirty white children with no manners "powhitetrash."
6. Marguerite made designs in the dirt with her rake.
7. Marguerite made fans before the children came.
8. Marguerite made concentric hearts with an arrow piercing them after the children came.
9. Mrs. Henderson stood with the upper part of her body erect and sang hymns while the powhitetrash taunted her.
10. Mrs. Henderson seemed happy with her behavior after the children left.

***Suggested Essay Topics***

1. Describe Mrs. Henderson's encounter with the powhitetrash. Why do you think Mrs. Henderson behaved as she did? What feelings do you think she had after the encounter?
2. What values did Mrs. Henderson teach her grandchildren? Do you think these values were the same as those taught in the homes of the powhitetrash? Explain your answer.

# Chapter 6

New Characters:

**Reverend Howard Thomas:** *the presiding elder*

**Reverend Taylor:** *the pastor of the church*

**Sister Monroe:** *a church member who often "gets the spirit"*

**Deacon Jackson:** *a church member who gets involved in a church scene*

**Sister Willson:** *in charge of the ushers and gets involved in the scene*

***Summary***

Chapter 6 describes both the visits of the Reverend Howard Thomas to the home of Mrs. Henderson and the humorous events within a special church service. Marguerite and Bailey dislike the visits of Reverend Thomas because he eats the best parts of the chicken at Sunday dinner. At one of the church services when Reverend Thomas visits Reverend Taylor's church, Sister Monroe "gets the spirit" and attacks Reverend Taylor; all the while she screams, "Preach it." Deacon Jackson and Sister Willson join the fray as they try to control Sister Monroe. Reverend Thomas manages to outstep her, but she finally hits him and his teeth fly out. When Marguerite and Bailey become hysterical with laughter, Uncle Willie takes them outside and gives them the whipping of their lives. For weeks after, Bailey would try to get Marguerite to laugh again by whispering, "Preach it!"

***Analysis***

The children are maturing and assuming more responsibility, but they still often misbehave and are treated like children. For instance, Uncle Willie confronts and punishes the children when they act up in church. The difficulties they still have in controlling themselves is evident when both Bailey and Marguerite lose control and howl with laughter during the preaching service; Marguerite describes how she "cried and hollered, passed gas and urine."

Angelou helps the reader to visualize the visit of Reverend Thomas and the church service when the children roll with laughter. Personification is used to describe his teeth jumping from his mouth. Imagery helps one see the "Elder Thomas with his lips flapping" and connotation helps the reader visualize the "grinning uppers and lowers" lying by Marguerite's foot. The writer uses the repetition of "I say, preach it!" to add humor to the sketch. Marguerite's narration presents a sketch of a preaching service as humorous as that depicted by Mark Twain in *Tom Sawyer* when he tells of a dog entering the church.

***Study Questions***

1. Who was the presiding elder over the district that included Stamps?
2. How often did the elder visit Marguerite's church?
3. What was the main reason for Marguerite's hatred of the preacher?
4. What was the good thing about the elder's visit?
5. What did Marguerite do instead of going up to the preacher?
6. What happened to Marguerite and Bailey after they laughed in church?
7. What spoiled the breakfast on the mornings the preacher stayed with them?
8. Where did Marguerite and Bailey sit in church when the church elder came?
9. Why was Deuteronomy Marguerite's favorite book of the Bible?
10. Who was the woman who caused problems in the church service?

***Answers***

1. The Reverend Thomas was the presiding elder over the district that included Stamps.
2. The elder visited Marguerite's church every three months.
3. Marguerite did not like the preacher because he got the best piece of chicken every time.
4. The good thing about the visit was that he did not come until after supper on Saturday night.
5. Marguerite cried instead of going up to the preacher.
6. Marguerite and Bailey received the whipping of their lives from Uncle Willie.
7. The preacher prayed so long the food became cold.

8. Marguerite and Bailey sat on the front row on the mourner's bench.
9. Marguerite liked Deuteronomy because she hoped that she could follow all the rules to avoid hell and brimstone.
10. Sister Monroe caused the problems in the church service.

***Suggested Essay Topics***

1. Describe Reverend Thomas. What were Marguerite's feelings about the Reverend Thomas? Why would she not shake hands with him?
2. The narrator in Chapter 6 is very young. What evidence do you have that she is an innocent child? How does her innocence affect what is told in this chapter? Give examples.

# Chapter 7

New Characters:

**Mr. Johnson:** *Mrs. Henderson's first husband and the grandfather of Marguerite*

**Mr. Henderson:** *Mrs. Annie Henderson's second husband*

**Mr. Murphy:** *Mrs. Henderson's third husband*

**Judge:** *makes "a gaffe calling a Negro woman Mrs. . . . "*

**Accused:** *hides behind Mrs. Henderson's chiffarobe*

***Summary***

Chapter 7 introduces the reader to Mrs. Henderson's three husbands—Mr. Johnson, Mr. Henderson, and Mr. Murphy. Marguerite tells the story of the judge who asks for the witness who hid the accused behind her chiffarobe; not knowing that "a woman who owned a store . . . would turn out to be colored," he asks for Mrs. Henderson. Mrs. Henderson turns out to be the only woman in Stamps referred to as "Mrs." by a white person.

### *Analysis*

To enhance her writing, Angelou employs stylistic devices. There is connotation in the simile "wore a snap-brim hat like George Raft." The reader would have to know the George Raft of movie-fame to understand the connotation in this phrase. Imagery helps the reader visualize the actions depicted in the chapter; for instance, "she laid down her handbag and slowly folded her handkerchief." The idiom is used in "The whites tickled their funny bones."

The theme of maturation is evident in Chapter 7 as Marguerite, still young and innocent, depicts the segregated world of Stamps to the reader through her young eyes.

### *Study Questions*

1. When did Mrs. Henderson marry Mr. Johnson?
2. On what subject would Mrs. Henderson give direct answers?
3. Who was Mrs. Henderson's last husband?
4. Who was Mrs. Henderson's second husband?
5. Who was Mrs. Henderson's first husband?
6. Did Mrs. Henderson think that "whitefolks" could be talked to safely and reasonably?
7. Name one instance of discrimination you see in Chapter 7.
8. Why do you think Mrs. Henderson acted surprised each Sunday when she was called on to lead the singing?
9. How did "the Negroes" react to the judge's calling Mrs. Henderson by the title "Mrs."?
10. Where did Mr. Murphy sleep when he came through the last time?

### *Answers*

1. Mrs. Henderson married Mr. Johnson around the turn of the century.
2. Mrs. Henderson would give direct answers on the subject of religion.

3. Mrs. Henderson's last husband was Mr. Murphy.
4. Mrs. Henderson's second husband was Mr. Henderson.
5. Mrs. Henderson's first husband was Mr. Johnson.
6. Mrs. Henderson believed that one risked his/her life to talk with "whitefolks."
7. When the judge called "a Negro woman Mrs.," everyone was surprised because titles were not given to "the Negroes." Another evidence of discrimination was not thinking "a Negro" could own a store. The segregated worship services were other examples of discrimination.
8. Mrs. Henderson acted surprised to appear humble, not vain or confident in being called upon to lead the singing.
9. They thought it proved "the worth and majesty of my grandmother."
10. Mr. Murphy slept on a pallet.

***Suggested Essay Topics***

1. How did Mrs. Henderson react when she was called on to lead a hymn? What do you think these motions and movements mean?
2. Describe the incident when Momma was called "Mrs." by the judge. What is the symbolism in the story? How do whites react to the story? How do Negroes react to the story, according to Marguerite?

# Chapter 8

***Summary***

Chapter 8 is a description of the caste system in Stamps, Arkansas, in the 1930s. Marguerite gives her views of the Depression, the actions of the people of Stamps, Mrs. Henderson, and the welfare agencies. She describes in detail how her grandmother works out a system of trade at the Store for the free commodities secured by area residents. Marguerite also tells about the Christmas gifts that arrive from their parents and the heartbreak that comes after they open them; until this time the children had not allowed themselves to think about why their parents had sent them away. The children tear the stuffing out of the doll, but they save the tea set in case their parents return.

***Analysis***

Marguerite and Bailey have matured to the point that they are beginning to question—but not understand—why their parents sent them to Stamps. When the Christmas gifts arrive, they do not express the happiness that often accompanies gifts and presents. Mrs. Henderson threatens to send the gifts back to their parents. "A wretched feeling of being torn engulfed me. I wanted to scream, 'Yes. Tell him to take them back.' But I didn't move."

Marguerite is better able to express her feelings about the caste system in Stamps: "A light shade had been pulled down between the Black community and all things white." Maya Angelou helps the reader to realize just how prejudiced Stamps was when she says that "the whites in our town were so prejudiced that a Negro couldn't buy vanilla ice cream." Then—to add humor—she adds "Except on July Fourth."

The metaphors used in Chapter 8 also illustrate the character-against-society conflict in Stamps. She tells the reader that "Stamps, Arkansas, was Chitlin' Switch, Georgia; Hang 'Em High, Alabama; Don't Let the Sun Set on You Here, Nigger, Mississippi." Marguerite realizes that Stamps is like many other racially segregated towns in the South of the 1930s.

***Study Questions***

1. How were Stamps, Arkansas, and Chitlin' Switch, Georgia, alike?
2. What did the writer mean when she said "a Negro couldn't buy vanilla ice cream"?
3. What was the difference between giving "in the Negro neighborhood" and the giving done by the whites?
4. What color, according to Marguerite, was God?

5. When did the "Negro community" finally realize that the Depression had come to Stamps?
6. Why did the people quit raising hogs?
7. How did Mrs. Henderson keep the Store going when the people of the community had only food from the welfare agencies instead of money?
8. Why did Marguerite think Uncle Willie was vain?
9. Why did Marguerite and Bailey eat the powdered eggs from the welfare when their family was not on welfare?
10. What did the children receive from their father on that "terrible Christmas"?

***Answers***

1. Both towns contained prejudiced people. Segregation and prejudice seemed to be a way of life in the Depression-era South.
2. The white people were so prejudiced that they would not allow "a Negro" to buy ice cream that was white. The ways of the segregated South of the 1930s were deeply set and would be hard to change.
3. "In the Negro neighborhood" a gift that was given was probably as desperately needed by the one who gave as by the one who received; whites, on the other hand, could spend money lavishly—according to Marguerite's way of thinking.
4. According to Marguerite, God was white.
5. The "Negro community" knew the Depression had come when cotton dropped from ten cents to eight, to seven, and finally to five cents.
6. The people quit trying to raise hogs because they could not afford to buy food for them.
7. Mrs. Henderson kept the Store going by allowing the people to use their powdered milk, powdered eggs, and cans of mackerel for trade in the store.

8. Marguerite thought Uncle Willie was vain when she had to iron seven starched white shirts and not iron any wrinkles into the material.
9. Marguerite and Bailey had to eat the eggs because Mrs. Henderson took them for trade and most people would trade them (not buy or eat the eggs themselves) because they tasted so bad.
10. The children's father sent them a picture of himself.

***Suggested Essay Topics***

1. What did the children receive for Christmas? How did they feel about the gifts? What were some of the questions the gifts raised for them?
2. Describe the feelings that Marguerite had toward the white "things." Why do you think that Marguerite had mixed feelings?

# Chapter 9

New Characters:

**Bailey Henderson, Sr.:** *the father of Marguerite and Bailey and the son of Mrs. Henderson*

**Vivian Baxter:** *the mother of the children; known as Mother Dear to Bailey, Jr.*

***Summary***

Bailey Henderson, Sr., comes to visit for a short while in Stamps. When he leaves, he takes Bailey and Marguerite with him. The children think that they are going to California, but he takes them to St. Louis, where their mother lives. Bailey Henderson, Sr., goes on to California, but he leaves the children with their mother. Marguerite thinks her mother is the most beautiful woman she has ever seen; Bailey falls instantly in love with her.

### *Analysis*

Marguerite is maturing and beginning to develop a poor self-concept. Marguerite finds it hard to wait for the children in town to find out her father is here. She wants them to know how handsome and wonderful he is, but when she thinks of being compared with him, she fears she will come up wanting. Bailey Henderson, Sr., makes fun of Marguerite on occasion and causes Marguerite to be pitted against him. Marguerite feels her father watching her; she feels so inferior to him that she wishes she "could grow small like Tiny Tim."

Marguerite struggles to accept herself and her body even though she feels inferior to others. When she meets her mother again, she is acutely aware of her own shortcomings. "I knew immediately why she sent me away. She was too beautiful to have children . . . They both had physical beauty."

Marguerite is unsure of herself and struggles to decide if she should go with her father or if she should stay with her grandmother. The reader also feels Marguerite's self-conflict when she writes: "Now this way, now that, now the other. Should I go with my father? Should I throw myself into the pond, and not being able to swim, join the body of . . . the boy who had drowned last summer? I couldn't decide on any move."

### *Study Questions*

1. What kind of car did Marguerite and Bailey's father drive?
2. What had been their father's job?
3. Why did Marguerite not want anyone to see her father?
4. How did Marguerite feel when her father watched her?
5. In later years Marguerite asked Mrs. Henderson, "Do you love me?" How did Mrs. Henderson respond?
6. How did Marguerite feel about leaving with her father?
7. Where did their mother live?
8. What "secret" language did Bailey and Marguerite speak?
9. How did Marguerite's father treat her, according to Marguerite?

10. How did Bailey react to his mother?

### *Answers*

1. Their father drove a DeSoto.
2. He had been a doorman at Santa Monica's plush Breakers Hotel.
3. Marguerite did not want anyone to see her father because she did not want to be compared to him; she felt she would come short.
4. Marguerite felt afraid when her father watched her.
5. Marguerite's grandmother said, "God is love. Just worry about whether you're being a good girl, then He will love you."
6. Marguerite could not make up her mind. She wanted to go with Bailey, but she wanted stay with her grandmother also.
7. Their mother lived in St. Louis.
8. Marguerite and Bailey spoke Pig Latin.
9. Marguerite felt her father favored Bailey over her. She felt he made fun of her and rejected her.
10. Bailey fell instantly and forever in love.

### *Suggested Essay Topics*

1. Describe Bailey Henderson, Sr., as he appeared to Marguerite. Do you see any weaknesses in Bailey Henderson, Sr.? Do you see any strengths in him? Explain.
2. Describe Marguerite's grandmother. Do you see any weaknesses in her? What are her greatest strengths? Explain.

# Chapter 10

New Characters:

**Grandmother Baxter:** *Marguerite's "nearly white" grandmother in St. Louis*

**Tutti, Tom, and Ira Baxter:** *Mother Dear's brothers and Marguerite's uncles*

**Pat Patterson:** *curses Vivian and is attacked by Vivian and her brothers*

**Mr. Freeman:** *Mother Dear's (Vivian's) live-in boyfriend*

### *Summary*

Chapter 10 describes the new people, places, and schoolrooms of St. Louis. The children hear family stories they have never heard before; for instance, they hear the story of how Mother ("Bibbi") is cursed by Pat Patterson and how the brothers find and hold him while "Bibbi" hits him with a club.

The social structure of St. Louis is a marked contrast to Stamps, Arkansas. Marguerite realizes early in their acquaintance that her grandmother is a precinct captain with power. Marguerite is able to deduce through the stories of the tough brothers that the positions they hold in the town have been bought through their actions.

The children are getting along well in their new school and accept their mother's live-in boyfriend as their father.

### *Analysis*

Conflict is a way of life in St. Louis. For instance, Bibbi herself brings physical violence against Pat Patterson. Character-against-society conflict is most evident as the children try to adapt to a new way of living; Bailey, in particular, has to learn a way of "in-fighting, Bailey style" in order to survive.

Maya Angelou helps the reader to visualize the characters. Imagery helps us to picture Mother: "a pretty woman, light-skinned with straight hair." The simile "like a pretty kite that floated just above my head" gives the reader a feeling of the elusive quality of

Mother. Onomatopoeia is illustrated with words like "sizzling" and "siddity." Humor is used when Bailey tells Marguerite in a fight to "grab for the balls right away." He does not reply when Marguerite asks him what to do if she is fighting a girl.

Maturation is an important theme in Chapter 10. Marguerite and Bailey are learning to adapt to the new school, the new teacher, and the new classmates in their own ways; this adaptation is a sign of their maturation.

***Study Questions***

1. Grandmother Baxter is described as being a quadroon or an octoroon. What does this mean in Marguerite's language?
2. What career did Grandmother Baxter study after coming to St. Louis?
3. From where did Marguerite think the men on the street corners had taken their names?
4. What office did Grandmother Baxter hold which gave her power?
5. What did Marguerite think was the best thing the city had to offer?
6. How did the children do academically after coming to St. Louis?
7. What was Louie's?
8. How did Marguerite compare the teachers in Stamps with those in St. Louis?
9. What did Mother's brothers call her?
10. Who was Marguerite's favorite uncle?

***Answers***

1. Marguerite said that her grandmother was nearly white.
2. Grandmother Baxter studied nursing after coming to St. Louis.
3. Marguerite thought that the men on the streets had gotten their colorful names from Wild West books.

4. Grandmother Baxter was precinct captain; this gave her power.
5. Marguerite thought the best thing the city had to offer was peanuts mixed with jelly beans.
6. Marguerite and Bailey were advanced a grade because they were ahead of their peers, and the teachers did not want the country children to put the others to shame.
7. Louie's was a long, dark tavern at the end of the bridge near the school; it was owned by two Syrian brothers.
8. Marguerite thought the teachers were more formal than those in Stamps; they didn't whip the children with switches; they gave them licks on the hands with rulers; they were not as friendly as those in Stamps.
9. Mother's brothers called her Bibbi.
10. Marguerite's favorite uncle was Tommy.

### *Suggested Essay Topics*

1. Compare and contrast the schools, the classmates, the curriculum and the teachers that Marguerite and Bailey are accustomed to in Stamps with those they find in St. Louis.
2. Describe Grandmother Baxter in appearance and in personality. Compare and contrast her with Marguerite's other grandmother, Mrs. Annie Henderson.

## Chapter 11

### *Summary*

Marguerite begins to spend her hours out of school with books and radio programs. She rarely sees her mother; if Mother comes home before the children are in bed, Mother sends them to their rooms so she can spend time with Mr. Freeman. Marguerite says that she feels that she has again arrived in a place where she has not "come to stay."

Both children begin to have problems: Bailey begins to stutter

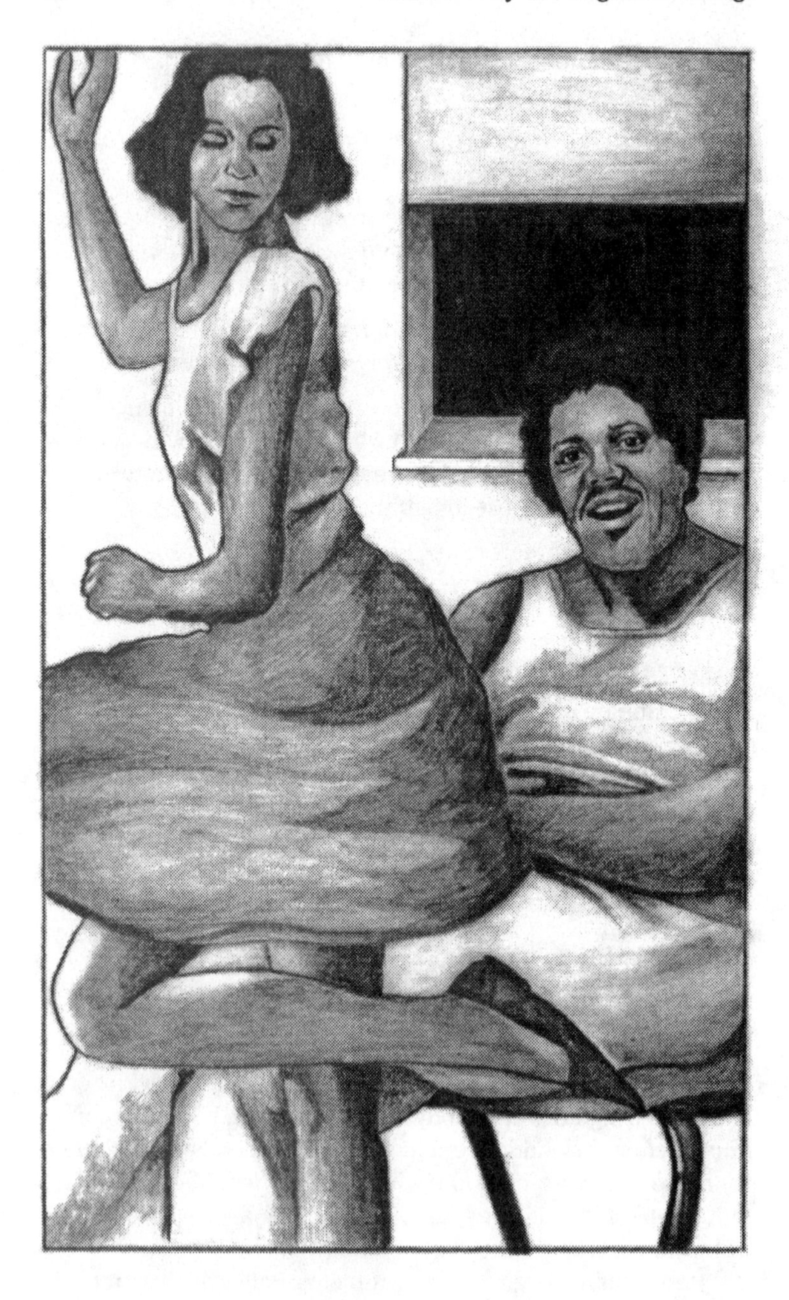

and Marguerite begins to have bad dreams. Marguerite goes into the bed of her mother (and Mr. Freeman) for comfort when the dreams occur.

On one of the occasions when Marguerite comes to their bed and Vivian goes to work, Mr. Freeman holds Marguerite and masturbates. Mr. Freeman threatens to kill Bailey if Marguerite ever tells what happened. Marguerite does not understand what has transpired. She only knows that it was good to be held.

Marguerite withdraws even more. She takes out a library card and begins to spend more time reading and less time with Bailey.

***Analysis***

Marguerite becomes very unsure of herself. She fears that Mr. Freeman will kill Bailey. She wants to ask what has happened but does not because she "knew when to keep quiet around adults." Even more conflict is apparent as Mr. Freeman tries to hide his actions from others and tells Marguerite never to tell "what they did."

Angelou helps the reader experience what Marguerite saw and felt: "He held me so softly that I wished he wouldn't ever let me go." The reader realizes the childishness and innocence of young Marguerite through the following simile: "I felt as sorry for him as I had felt for a litter of helpless pigs . . . " Connotation is used when the reader is told that Mr. Freeman's organ "stood up like a brown ear of corn" and that it "was mushy and squirmy like the inside of a freshly killed chicken." The reader is impressed with the innocence of Marguerite.

Although in the previous chapter it seemed that the children were maturing, in Chapter 11 Marguerite strikes the reader as still being very young, vulnerable, and innocent. Her innocence makes the crime against her even more horrible. Her withdrawal into books to protect herself against her thoughts and to prevent herself from sharing the terrible secret with others is her way of coping.

***Study Questions***

1. What shield helped Marguerite to survive in St. Louis?

2. What did it mean when Marguerite says that she sneaked away to Robin Hood's forest?
3. What was the honor system the children had with their mother?
4. What difficulty did Bailey begin to experience in St. Louis?
5. What difficulty did Marguerite begin to experience in St. Louis?
6. What directions did Mother give the children every night?
7. How did Marguerite feel about being held by Mr. Freeman?
8. Who did Marguerite think was the greatest writer in the world?
9. What threat did Mr. Freeman make?
10. What was the first secret that Marguerite ever kept from Bailey?

*Answers*

1. Marguerite tries to cope with her life in St. Louis by telling herself that she had really not come to stay. In this way she managed to survive St. Louis.
2. Marguerite was withdrawing into fantasy; she was pretending that she was in the woods of the folklore character Robin Hood whom she had read about.
3. Marguerite and Bailey had to do their homework, eat dinner and wash their dishes before they could listen to the radio; since no one was there to check on them, they had to be honest about it themselves.
4. Bailey began to stutter in St. Louis.
5. Marguerite began to have bad dreams in St. Louis.
6. Marguerite and Bailey were advised by their mother every night to say their prayers and to go to bed.
7. Marguerite liked being held by Mr. Freeman; she felt that she had found a safe home and that he would never let anything happen to her.

8. Marguerite thought that Horatio Alger was the greatest writer in the world.
9. Mr. Freeman threatened to kill Bailey if she ever told.
10. Marguerite's first secret from Bailey was what had happened between Mr. Freeman and her.

### *Suggested Essay Topics*

1. What was Marguerite's routine after school each day? Compare and contrast this routine to her after-school routine in Stamps.
2. Describe how Marguerite copes with her life in St. Louis and with the secrets Mr. Freeman forces her to keep.

# Chapter 12

### *Summary*

One Saturday in late spring while Vivian is at work and Bailey is playing baseball, Mr. Freeman rapes Marguerite. After the rape, he bathes Marguerite and tells her never to tell what happened or he will kill Bailey. He tells the eight-year-old to go to the library. The pain is so intense that Marguerite does not stay long. She returns home and goes immediately to bed.

Vivian and Mr. Freeman quarrel during the night. The next morning Mr. Freeman leaves. Marguerite is unable to leave her bed. A doctor is called, but he does not discover the reason that Marguerite is ill. Through a haze, Marguerite realizes that Mother and Bailey are caring for her. The chapter concludes with Marguerite's stained panties falling at her mother's feet.

### *Analysis*

The rape in Chapter 12 brings conflict and grief to Marguerite along with the end of Marguerite's innocence. Marguerite states that she could not "sit long on the hard seats in the library (they had been constructed for children)." She hints at the end of her childhood through this reference to the benches.

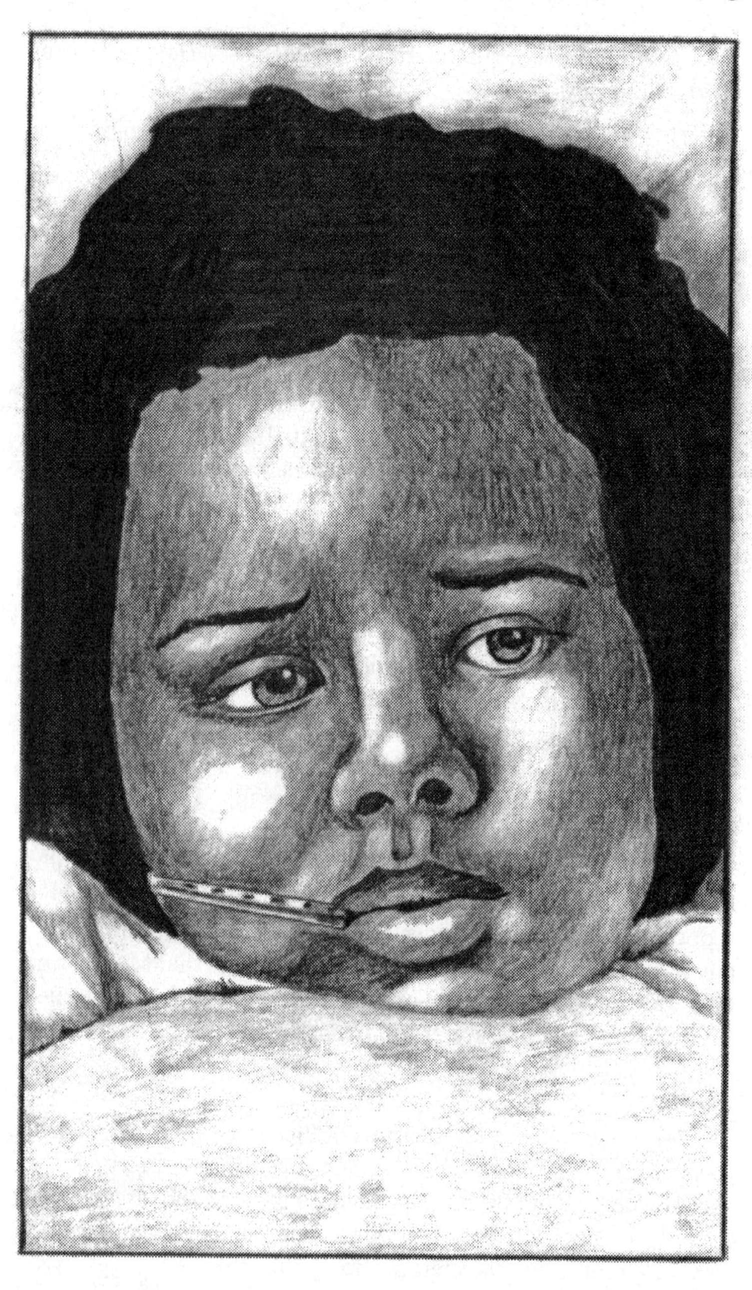

Marguerite struggles not to scream during the rape since Mr. Freeman has told her he will kill her if she makes any noise; her young, innocent body has to yield to his adult attack. Later Marguerite struggles with herself not to tell anyone that her body has been ravaged by Mr. Freeman's abuse for fear that Mr. Freeman will kill Bailey.

***Study Questions***

1. Where was Bailey when the rape occurred?
2. Who did Marguerite expect to come in while she was being raped?
3. How old was Marguerite when she was raped?
4. What book or comic strip did Bailey read to Marguerite while she was sick?
5. How did Mother know of the rape?
6. Why did Marguerite want to leave?
7. What was Mother fixing Marguerite for breakfast?
8. Where did Mr. Freeman send Marguerite after he raped her?
9. What did Mr. Freeman say he would do if Marguerite screamed as he raped her?
10. What did Mr. Freeman say he would do if Marguerite told what had happened?

***Answers***

1. Bailey was playing baseball when the rape occurred.
2. Marguerite expected Bailey, her mother or the Green Hornet to come in while the rape was occurring.
3. Marguerite was eight when she was raped.
4. Bailey read the *Rover Boys* and *The Katzenjammer Kids* to Marguerite while she was sick.
5. Mother found the stained panties at her feet when Bailey helped to change the bed.

6. Marguerite knew she was dying and she wanted to go away because she did not want to die near Mr. Freeman.
7. Mother was fixing Marguerite some Cream of Wheat.
8. Mr. Freeman sent Marguerite to the library after he raped her.
9. Mr. Freeman said he would kill Marguerite if she screamed.
10. Mr. Freeman said he would kill Bailey if Marguerite told.

***Suggested Essay Topics***

1. Marguerite tries to escape in different ways from her life in St. Louis. Describe these ways and explain them.
2. Describe Marguerite's feelings and thoughts while she was "sick." Why did she have these feelings and thoughts?

## Chapter 13

***Summary***

Marguerite is hospitalized—a not unpleasant experience for her. She relishes the attention given to her by the adults around her.

When Mr. Freeman goes to trial, Marguerite agrees to testify for two reasons: Bailey says it would prevent another little girl from being hurt and he promises Marguerite that Mr. Freeman will not be able to kill him. Marguerite does not testify about the times that Mr. Freeman held her and masturbated; this causes her guilt.

Mr. Freeman is given one year and one day, but for some reason he is released that afternoon. The police come to the home of Grandmother Baxter and tell her that Mr. Freeman "has been found dead on the lot behind the slaughterhouse." It is clear to even young Marguerite which St. Louis family was powerful enough to secure Mr. Freeman's release and which family was capable of murdering him.

Marguerite copes with the rape and all that has happened by refusing to talk. She believes if she talks with "anyone else that person might die too." At first, "they" understood her silence. Next, the adults try punishment to get her to talk. Finally they banish Marguerite and Bailey to Stamps.

***Analysis***

Through characterization, the reader knows and cares for Marguerite and her family. Person-against-person conflict is first evident when Marguerite testifies against Mr. Freeman; it occurs also when the uncles pit themselves against him. Character-against-self conflict is evident when Marguerite struggles on the stand not to tell the whole truth about her relationship with Mr. Freeman. When the uncles take revenge on Mr. Freeman instead of leaving it to the justice system, character-against-society conflict is evident.

It is interesting that in this autobiography so carefully penned there are definite—though minor—inconsistencies. Marguerite says at one point at the beginning of the chapter that Bailey cried at her hospital bedside and that he did not cry again for 15 years; at the end of the chapter, however, she tells of Bailey's crying his heart out down the aisles of the coach as they return to Stamps. It is unclear whether this is a mistake or an exaggeration; in any case it is confusing to the reader.

Marguerite's innocence is stolen from her; this is particularly evident in Chapter 13 of this autobiography. For instance, Marguerite states that after the rape, "I was eight, and grown." It seems to Marguerite that she will never be a carefree child again.

***Study Questions***

1. What did Bailey tell Marguerite that she must do in the courtroom?
2. Why did he say that Marguerite must do this in the courtroom?
3. Why did Marguerite believe Bailey when he said that he would not let Mr. Freeman kill him?
4. How did Marguerite feel about the hospital?
5. Why did Marguerite's uncles not harm Mr. Freeman immediately when they found out what he had done?

6. Marguerite compares excitement to what?
7. How did Marguerite lie on the witness stand?
8. What was Mr. Freeman's sentence?
9. What did the police officer say happened to Mr. Freeman?
10. What were Grandmother Baxter's directions about the death of Mr. Freeman?

***Answers***

1. Bailey said that Marguerite must tell what Mr. Freeman did to her when she was called upon to testify.
2. Bailey said that Marguerite must tell the truth to keep another little girl from being hurt.
3. Marguerite believed Bailey because he never lied to her.
4. Marguerite loved the hospital and would have liked to have stayed there.
5. Marguerite's uncles did not harm Mr. Freeman because he was arrested.
6. Marguerite compared excitement to a drug.
7. Marguerite lied on the witness stand because she did not tell about Mr. Freeman's advances to her before the rape.
8. Mr. Freeman's sentence was one year and one day.
9. Mr. Freeman had been found dead in the slaughterhouse lot. He looked as if he had been kicked to death.
10. Grandmother Baxter said that Bailey and Marguerite must never mention the name of Mr. Freeman or the situation again.

***Suggested Essay Topics***

1. How was Marguerite able to deal with what had happened to her?
2. How did Bailey react to Marguerite's rape? Why did he react in this way? How did the nurses react to the rape? How did other adults about her react to the rape and to Marguerite's muteness?

# Chapter 14

### *Summary*

Marguerite and Bailey return to Stamps, Arkansas, after the trial; Marguerite finds the "barrenness of Stamps was exactly what I wanted." The community receives the children well: the people listen to Bailey's stories and seem to accept Marguerite's muteness. Marguerite concludes that she "was not so much forgiven as I was understood."

### *Analysis*

Bailey plays "on the country folks' need for diversion" and attacks them with words and tall tales—despite Mrs. Henderson's reminder to tell the truth. As Marguerite tries to cope with what happened to her, she tries to express her feelings and thoughts: "Sounds came to me dully, as if people were speaking through their handkerchiefs . . . Colors weren't true . . . I began to worry about my sanity."

Bailey is growing and maturing in body and in self-confidence. He is resentful, however, that he must return to the South. The reader feels, however, that Marguerite is waiting quietly for her physical and emotional wounds to heal; her maturation seems to be temporarily at a standstill. She feels understood in the Southern community and feels the barrenness of the small Southern town is just what she needs.

### *Study Questions*

1. How did Marguerite feel about the barrenness of Stamps?
2. How high did Bailey report that the buildings were in the North?
3. How did Bailey say that one could win a "zillion" dollars?
4. What dessert did Bailey say that they made in the North?
5. What term did Mrs. Annie Henderson use for a "lie"?
6. How did Bailey describe the Northern watermelons?
7. How did Marguerite feel among the people in Stamps?

8. What were the high spots in Stamps?
9. What was meant by a person being "tender-hearted"?
10. What did it mean when the customer said that Bailey had a silver tongue?

***Answers***

1. Marguerite felt that the barrenness of Stamps was just what she needed.
2. Bailey said that the buildings were so high that in the winter the people did not see the tops for months.
3. Bailey said one could win a zillion dollars if one could count the seeds in a watermelon before it was cut.
4. Marguerite and Bailey made snow ice cream from snow, sugar, and Pet milk.
5. Mrs. Annie Henderson called a lie a "not true."
6. Bailey said that the watermelons were twice as big as a cow's head and sweet as syrup.
7. Marguerite said that she felt not so much forgiven as she felt understood.
8. The high spots in Stamps were negative: droughts, lynchings, deaths, floods, and similar occurrences.
9. A tender-hearted person was a sensitive person; people who were tender-hearted were looked upon as being a little sick or in delicate health.
10. Bailey was said to have a silver tongue because he could easily tell stories; the stories rolled off his tongue smoothly and people tended to believe him.

***Suggested Essay Topics***

1. How did Bailey describe the North? Was it accurate? Explain. Why did he give the descriptions he did?
2. Why did the people in Stamps think that Marguerite was not talking? Was this the real reason for Marguerite's silence? Explain.

# Chapter 15

New Character:

**Mrs. Bertha Flowers:** *"the aristocrat of Black Stamps" and "the lady who threw me my first life line"*

### *Summary*

Marguerite sops around the house "like an old biscuit" until she is thrown a life line by Mrs. Flowers. Mrs. Flowers asks Marguerite to carry her groceries home. Margaret is thrilled that she has been asked to go and changes her clothes before they leave. When Mrs. Flowers comments on how professionally sewn the dress is, Mrs. Henderson makes Marguerite remove it so that Mrs. Flowers can see the seams. Marguerite is humiliated. Mrs. Flowers seems to understand Marguerite's feelings. She compliments Mrs. Henderson's sewing and tells Marguerite to dress again.

When Marguerite reaches Mrs. Flowers' home with the parcels, Mrs. Flowers invites her inside. She gives Marguerite cookies and challenges Marguerite with her "lessons for living." Before Marguerite returns to the Store, Mrs. Flowers lends her a book of poetry and asks her to recite at their next session.

When Marguerite arrives home, Mrs. Henderson hears her take the Lord's name in vain by saying, "By the way." Mrs. Henderson explains that "Jesus was the Way, the Truth, and the Light,' and anyone who says 'by the way' is really saying 'by Jesus' or 'by God." Marguerite is whipped and reminded that whitefolks use "by the way" often. Mrs. Henderson explains the mouths of white people "were most in general loose and their words were an abomination before Christ."

### *Analysis*

The reader senses that Mrs. Flowers' invitation to come inside may have been planned by Mrs. Henderson and Mrs. Flowers during one of their conversations. Maya Angelou makes use of several stylistic devices in describing Mrs. Flowers and Marguerite's visit to her home. "The sweet scent of vanilla had met us as she opened the door" is an example of personification. The reader hears and sees Mrs. Flowers through the metaphor "her reading was a won-

der in my ears" and through the simile "like a plum if snagged." Angelou uses dialect when she quotes Mrs. Henderson as saying, "How you, Sister Flowers?" The imagery makes the sights, smells, and feelings real to the audience; for example, Angelou vividly describes the cookies: "They were flat round wafers, slightly browned on the edges and butter-yellow in the center." Connotation, another stylistic device, is evident in the phrase, "sweetmilk fresh."

Marguerite is still struggling with accepting the rape, her own identity, and her growing maturity. She is becoming more aware of her body. For example, when Mrs. Henderson tells Marguerite to remove her dress so Mrs. Flowers can see the carefully stitched seams, Marguerite is terrified.

The secondary motif of education is important to Chapter 15 as Mrs. Flowers teaches Marguerite many lessons. These include the fact that the human voice is necessary to infuse words with meanings, that one should be intolerant of ignorance but understanding of illiteracy, and that some people unable to go to school are actually more educated and intelligent than college professors. Mrs. Flowers has indeed become Marguerite's "life line."

***Study Questions***

1. Who was the person who helped Marguerite stop "sopping around the house . . . like an old biscuit"?
2. Why did Mrs. Flowers appeal to Marguerite?
3. Why was it fortunate that Marguerite never saw Mrs. Flowers in the company of powhitefolks?
4. Why was Marguerite—not Bailey—sent home with Mrs. Flowers?
5. What was the reason that a child would go home from the Store with Mrs. Flowers?
6. Why did Mrs. Henderson make Marguerite take off her dress in front of Mrs. Flowers?
7. Why did Marguerite not protest taking her dress off in front of Mrs. Flowers?

8. What did Mrs. Flowers say separated the animals from people?
9. What did Mrs. Flowers lend to Marguerite?
10. What did Mrs. Flowers give Marguerite to eat?

*Answers*

1. Mrs. Flowers helped Marguerite to stop sopping around like a biscuit.
2. Mrs. Flowers appealed to Marguerite because she was like people that Marguerite had never met personally; she was like women in English novels who walked the moors, who drank tea in front of roaring fireplaces, who walked the "heath" and read morocco-bound books, who had two last names divided by a hyphen. She was like people Marguerite dreamed of becoming.
3. Marguerite was probably fortunate in never seeing Mrs. Flowers with the powhitetrash because they probably would have spoken to her commonly and called her Bertha. Marguerite would have had to admit that Mrs. Flowers was a real person, a human being with frailties.
4. Mrs. Flowers asked that Marguerite—not Bailey—go with her. This visit, the reader senses, may have been planned by Mrs. Henderson and Mrs. Flowers.
5. A child was sent home from the store with Mrs. Flowers to help her carry her purchases.
6. Marguerite had to take off her dress so that Mrs. Henderson could show Mrs. Flowers her needlework.
7. Marguerite was afraid that if she protested her grandmother would think she was womanish; she also thought it would remind her grandmother of what had happened in St. Louis.
8. Mrs. Flowers said that language separated the animals from people.
9. Mrs. Flowers gave Marguerite a book of poems to take home with her.

10. Mrs. Flowers gave Marguerite some cookies to eat and lemonade to drink.

***Suggested Essay Topics***

1. How did Marguerite feel about Mrs. Flowers? Why did she feel this way?
2. What were the lessons that Mrs. Flowers gave to Marguerite? Which lesson do you think was most important for Marguerite at this time?

# Chapter 16

New Characters:

**Mrs. Viola Cullinan:** *Marguerite's employer*

**Miss Glory:** *the cook who also works for Miss Cullinan*

***Summary***

Chapter 16 describes the preparations for life given girls in the South. "While white girls learned to waltz and sit gracefully with a tea cup balanced . . . we were lagging behind, learning the mid-Victorian values." Another preparation for life given to Black Southern girls is working in the kitchen or home of a white family. Ten-year-old Marguerite enrolls in this "finishing school" when she becomes an employee of Mrs. Cullinan.

Marguerite overhears her employer and guest talking about her. During the course of the conversation, she hears the guest remark that "her name's too long. I'd never bother myself. I'd call her Mary if I was you." Marguerite becomes very angry and feels her "lunch in her mouth a second time." The next day, Mrs. Cullinan calls her by the shortened name. Marguerite explained that "Every person I knew had a hellish horror of being "called out of his name."

Marguerite becomes angry. She longs to quit the job, but she knows that her grandmother will not allow her to do so. She and Bailey devise a plan to get Marguerite fired; Marguerite breaks some of Mrs. Cullinan's favorite dishes. Mrs. Cullinan falls on the floor and cries.

After Marguerite has carried out the plan, she is able to return to the Store and her family. She is never able, however, to tell Bailey all about the incident because she always begins to laugh.

***Analysis***

Racism is made very real in Chapter 16. When Miss Glory reminds Mrs. Cullinan that Marguerite's name is not Mary, Mrs. Cullinan replies that the name is "too long. She's Mary from now on." Angelou explains that centuries of being called "niggers, jigs, dinges, blackbirds, crows, boots and spooks" had given every person she knew a horror of being called "anything that could be loosely construed as insulting." Mrs. Cullinan did not think this child even deserved the effort of being called by name.

Mrs. Cullinan's action results in conflict. For instance, Marguerite becomes angry when she hears Mrs. Cullinan talking about her and when Mrs. Cullinan "calls her out of her name." Marguerite decides to get even with Mrs. Cullinan by breaking some of Mrs. Cullinan's dishes.

Marguerite's employer refuses to call Marguerite anything but Mary. Marguerite reports not knowing whether to laugh or cry; Marguerite's anger prevents her from doing either. When she is at last able to carry out the plan to get herself fired, she is never able to describe it to Bailey: "each time I got to the part where she fell on the floor and screwed up her ugly face to cry, we burst out laughing."

Character-against-society is most evident as the white women talk and decide to shorten Marguerite's name to Mary; Marguerite is determined to keep her own identity and not to be "called out of her name." She is at last able to devise a plan to rescue herself from the "white, fat, old" woman and the white visitors who frequented there.

Maya Angelou helps the reader to visualize the characters and the Cullinan home. Imagery helps the reader see Mrs. Cullinan: "She was singularly unattractive until she smiled, and then the lines around her eyes and mouth which made her look perpetually dirty disappeared." Angelou uses a simile in "like the mask of an impish elf." She employs connotation in "her Alice-in-Wonderland house."

A metaphor is used in the following clause: "a white woman's kitchen became my finishing school."

Symbolism is also employed in Chapter 16. A visitor to the Cullinan home gives Marguerite the shortened name of Mary; Marguerite retaliates in her autobiography by allowing this woman to go without a name.

The reader finds Marguerite even more mature in Chapter 16; she is now 10 years old and has a job outside the home. Occasionally the child Marguerite creeps into the chapter, but the maturational theme is important to the chapter and the autobiographical story.

***Study Questions***

1. How old was Marguerite when she went to work in a white home?
2. Who was Marguerite's employer?
3. What was the cook's real name?
4. What did Mrs. Cullinan call the cook?
5. What did it mean when Marguerite said that her lunch was in her mouth a second time?
6. What did Marguerite do that angered her employer?
7. Why did Marguerite break the dishes?
8. Why did Marguerite begin to come to work late and leave early?
9. Why did Marguerite not explain to Bailey what happened?
10. Who helped Marguerite decide what to do about the work situation?

***Answers***

1. Marguerite was 10 when she went to work at Mrs. Cullinan's.
2. Marguerite's employer was Mrs. Cullinan.
3. The cook's real name was Hallelujah.
4. Mrs. Cullinan called Hallelujah by the name Miss Glory.

5. Marguerite meant that she vomited when she said her food was in her mouth a second time.
6. Marguerite angered Mrs. Cullinan by breaking a casserole shaped like a fish and also two green cups.
7. Marguerite broke the dishes so that she would be fired.
8. Marguerite came to work late and left early in hopes that she would be fired; she knew that her grandmother would not let her leave the job for just any reason.
9. Marguerite could not tell Bailey what happened because she burst out laughing each time she tried to tell him.
10. It was Bailey who helped Marguerite plan what to do to get fired.

***Suggested Essay Topics***

1. Discuss the implications of using the shortened name of Mary instead of Marguerite.
2. Compare and contrast the preparation for life given the "Negro girls in small Southern towns" with that given the rich white girls.

# Chapter 17

New Characters:

**Kay Francis:** *a movie star who reminds Bailey of his mother*

**Miz Jenkins:** *a neighbor who speaks to Mrs. Henderson and Marguerite as they walk to meet Bailey*

***Summary***

Chapter 17 describes Saturday nights at Marguerite's home and particularly the Saturday night when Bailey does not come home on time. The reason for his lateness is that he has sat through a movie again to see more of Kay Francis, a movie star who reminds him of his mother. Uncle Willie whips Bailey with a belt because of

his curfew violation. Sometime later Marguerite and Bailey are able to go together to see a film with Kay Francis. On the return, Bailey tears across the tracks just as a train passes. Marguerite is relieved to find him well after the train passes. The chapter ends in humor when Marguerite tells the reader that one year later Bailey does catch a train—and gets stranded in Baton Rouge.

***Analysis***

Bailey is maturing—and becoming more belligerent—but it is obvious that he misses his mother terribly. Bailey opposes his grandmother and his Uncle Willie by arriving home late and giving no reason for his lateness. His silence is a type of confrontation. Bailey refuses to cry out in pain when Uncle Willie whips his naked skin with a belt.

The two children engage in a conflict when they both attend a movie starring Kay Francis. "I laughed because, except that she was white, the big movie star looked just like my mother . . . And it was funny to think of the whitefolks' not knowing that the woman they were adoring could be my mother's twin, except that she was white and my mother was prettier."

Social realism is evident also in Chapter 17 in the description of the movie theatre with its "whitefolks downstairs" and the "Negroes in the buzzards' roost." This segregation and the contrived, stereotypical dialect in the movie give the reader a glimpse of the Southern town of Stamps.

***Study Questions***

1. What day was always different to Marguerite?
2. Why did the farmers stop at the Store on the way to town?
3. How did Uncle Willie try to entertain the children while their parents were inside the Store?
4. What did Bailey play with the older boys while their parents were inside?
5. What did Marguerite have for breakfast on Saturday?
6. How did the children shine Uncle Willie's shoes?

7. How did Bailey use his allowance?
8. How did Marguerite use her allowance?
9. Why did the store use electric lights on Saturdays?
10. Why was Mother Dear never mentioned to other people?

### *Answers*

1. Saturdays were always different to Marguerite.
2. Farmers were always stopping at the store to get change.
3. Uncle Willie tried to entertain the children by giving them bits of peanut patties which had been broken in shipment.
4. Bailey played mumbledypeg with the older boys.
5. Breakfast on Saturdays was usually dry cereal and fresh milk.
6. The children shined Uncle Willie's shoes with a biscuit.
7. Bailey used his money to go to the movie.
8. Marguerite gave Bailey her dime and he usually brought back Smith and Street cowboy books to her.
9. The electric lights were used so late shoppers could see that the Store was still open.
10. Mother Dear was never mentioned because there was not enough of her to share.

### *Suggested Essay Topics*

1. Compare and contrast Marguerite and Bailey's reaction to the movie with Kay Francis. Explain their silence about their discovery.
2. Describe the family's reactions to Bailey's curfew violation. Does it seem the family overreacted? Explain.

# Chapter 18

New Characters:

**Brother Stewart and Bishop, Mrs. Duncan, Sister Williams, Miss Grace:** *flat characters who appear in Chapter 18 to let the reader meet some cotton-pickers, revival team members, and worshipers at the tent revival*

### *Summary*

Chapter 18 describes in detail the cotton-pickers in the Store at the end of the day and the same cotton-pickers (and others) at the tent revival that night. The revival services in the cloth tent include members of all denominations. Included in the services are prayers, hymns, shouters, a sermon and a revolutionary action: a minister who takes in members for other churches. The collection comes last in the service and the revival members give from their small means. As the worshipers make their way home, they pass a honky-tonk. Both groups ask, "How long, oh God?"

### *Analysis*

Irony is present when the revival-goers pass a honky-tonk filled with merry-makers. Both groups, however, are victims of the discrimination of the South. They both ask, "How long, oh God?" Marguerite is very angry toward the system and toward the cotton-pickers who "have allowed themselves to be worked like oxen" and who struggle to survive a pitiful existence. Marguerite yearns "to tell them to stand up and 'assume the posture of a man.'"

A more mature Marguerite questions the lifestyles of those about her and the quiet acceptance of the hard work they endure. A secondary motif of religion is evident in Chapter 18; the reader sees firsthand the importance of the worship experience to young Marguerite and to the tired workers who muster enough energy after a day in the fields to attend worship services. The reader—and Marguerite—are still left with the question, "How long?"

### *Study Questions*

1. How did the cotton-pickers get to the fields?

2. Why did the workers go to the tent revival even though they were tired?
3. Why did the people not talk and ask questions before the revival?
4. How many people were saved that night?
5. Which denomination was considered "hoity-toity"?
6. Which denomination was considered intellectual?
7. Why did the people look with suspicion on the Church of God in Christ?
8. Why did the Church of God say that they behaved as they did?
9. What advertisement did Texarkana's largest Negro funeral home give out?
10. What revolutionary thing did the preacher at the tent revival do?

***Answers***

1. The workers got to the fields in a cotton truck.
2. Even though they were tired, the people went to the revival to feed their souls.
3. The people did not talk before the service because they were concerned with "the coming meeting, soul to soul, with God."
4. Twenty souls were saved during the revival.
5. Marguerite considered the Mount Zion Baptist Church to be hoity-toity.
6. The members of the African Methodist Episcopal and the African Methodist Episcopal Zion Churches were considered intellectuals.
7. The people looked with suspicion on the Church of God in Christ because they were noisy.

8. The people of the Church of God in Christ were noisy because the Bible said to make a joyful noise.
9. Cardboard fans were used for advertising purposes by Texarkana's largest Negro funeral home.
10. The preacher did something revolutionary when he took in members of other churches.

***Suggested Essay Topics***

1. Contrast religion in the life of the poor and downtrodden and in the life of the whites, according to Marguerite.
2. Contrast and compare the tent revival with the service Marguerite describes earlier in the book.

# Chapter 19

New Character:

**Joe Louis:** *the boxer, known as the Brown Bomber, who would become the Heavyweight Champion of the World*

***Summary***

Chapter 19 describes in detail the congregating of the community around the radio in the Store to listen to boxing matches. Men, women, and children come to listen and to buy soft drinks; in case of a particularly bloody fight, they also buy peanut patties and Baby Ruths. When Joe Louis becomes the Heavyweight Champion of the World, some people do not return home but stay overnight in town; they are afraid to be on a country road at night when Joe Louis has proved "we were the strongest people in the world."

***Analysis***

A maturing Marguerite is becoming more aware of the harshness of racial discrimination and the fear of the Black community toward whites. A Black fighter dares to compete for the title of Heavyweight Champion of the World. As Joe Louis represents his people and wins, his triumph is for blacks everywhere.

Dialect plays an important part in Chapter 19. The announcer shouts, "The winnah." He mentions "jabs," "a left cross," and difficulty in keeping "his block up." A simile is used in the phrase "as a black sky is streaked with lightning."

***Study Questions***

1. Why was the radio in the Store turned up as high as it would go?
2. Where did the children sit during the fight?
3. When would the real festivities in the Store begin?
4. Who came to listen to the fight?
5. Why did the coins lie on top of the cash register during the fight?
6. What type of company sponsored the fight?
7. What were some of the soft drinks sold at the store?
8. Whom did Joe Louis fight?
9. What candies were sold at the Store if the fight were particularly bloody?
10. What title did Joe Louis win?

***Answers***

1. The radio was high so that those on the porch could hear.
2. The children sat on any lap available or on the porch.
3. The real festivities would not begin until after the fight was over.
4. Everyone came to listen to the fight.
5. The coins were kept on top of the cash register until after the fight to prevent the jangle of the cash register from disturbing the fight.
6. A razor blade company sponsored the fight.
7. Some of the soft drinks sold were R.C. Colas, Dr. Peppers, Coca-Colas, and Hire's root beer.

8. Joe Louis and Camera fought.
9. Peanut patties and Baby Ruths were some of the candies sold.
10. Joe Louis became the Heavyweight Champion of the World.

***Suggested Essay Topics***

1. Describe the Store on the night of the fight for the Heavyweight Champion of the World. (Be sure to comment on the atmosphere before, during, and after the event.) Compare and contrast the Store on this night with the Store during a typical work day.
2. Joe Louis's fight represented something to the residents of Stamps who gathered at the Store. What was the symbolism involved in his winning? What would have been the symbolism had he lost? Would the people have behaved differently after the fight was over if Joe had lost? Explain your answer.

# Chapter 20

New Characters:

**Louise Kendricks:** *the "prettiest female in Stamps, next to Miss Flowers," and Marguerite's first friend*

**Tommy Valdon:** *Marguerite's suitor*

**Miss Williams:** *Marguerite's seventh-grade teacher*

**Helen Gray:** *a recipient of a Valentine and a very minor, flat character*

***Summary***

At the annual summer picnic fish fry Marguerite makes her first close, girl friend: Louise Kendricks. Marguerite also has her first interest in a boy; Tommy Valdon not only sends Marguerite a love note, but he also sends her a valentine which the teacher (Miss Williams) reads aloud to the whole class. Although Marguerite

MEN
WOMEN

determines to say something clever to him, she can never do anything but giggle when he is around.

***Analysis***

When the chapter opens, the reader finds Marguerite avoiding others. Marguerite plans to bring a book to read to the picnic, but her grandmother will not allow it. At the picnic Marguerite wanders away by herself. It is at this point that Louise finds her and a friendship ensues with Louise.

The theme of maturation is vital to the chapter; Marguerite says that in her new friendship "after being a woman for three years I was about to become a girl." The reader realizes that Marguerite is at last able to find joy after her return to Stamps. A new friendship makes all the difference in Marguerite's life. The pleasure of Louise's company makes Marguerite—and the reader—eager to continue.

Along with Louise, Marguerite finds that someone else is interested in her. Tommy Valdon sends her a note and a valentine. Marguerite wants "to say something extra nice" to Tommy but finds that "each time I saw Tommy I . . . was unable to form a coherent sentence."

Imagery helps the reader experience the picnic: "Pans of fried chicken, covered with dishtowels, sat under benches next to a mountain of potato salad crammed with hard-boiled eggs." The simile in the "recipe was guarded like a scandalous affair" indicates the importance attached to the dishes brought to the event. Onomatopoeic words like "sputtered" and "chugged" give sound and feeling to the picnic scene.

Metaphors like "a moment of green grass" and "raised a platform of my mind's eye" are examples of another device used by Angelou. The personification in "dresses dashed, stopped and darted" helps the reader form a mental image. Another important element in the chapter is dialect; for example, someone threatens, "Boys, don' chew let that ball fall on none of my cakes, you do and it'll be me on you."

Social realism is also important to Chapter 20. The reader experiences firsthand the social occasion of a picnic, the beginning of the friendship of two young girls, and the boy-girl relationships in seventh and eighth grades, an important part of maturing in Stamps society.

***Study Questions***

1. What was the biggest outdoor event of the year?
2. Name at least two social groups represented at the picnic.
3. What were some of the musical instruments found at the picnic?
4. How were the watermelons chilled at the picnic?
5. Why did Marguerite not bring a book to read?
6. Describe the bathroom facilities at the picnic.
7. Who was Marguerite's first real friend?
8. What was the signal for Marguerite and her friend to meet?
9. What did Miss Williams say was wrong with Tommy's valentine?
10. What language did the girls teach each other?

***Answers***

1. The biggest outdoor event of the year was the summer picnic.
2. Social groups represented at the picnic were the Elks, Eastern Star, Masons, Knights of Columbus, and Daughters of Pythias.
3. Musical instruments included "cigar-box guitars, harmonicas, juice harps, combs wrapped in tissue paper and even bathtub basses."
4. Watermelons were chilled by placing them in the Coca-Cola box and filling "all the tubs with ice as well as the big black wash pot."
5. Marguerite did not bring a book because her grandmother said if she did not play with the other children, she could clean fish, bring water or carry wood.

6. The bathroom facilities were actually just paths going into the woods.
7. Marguerite's first real friend was named Louise Kendricks.
8. Marguerite and Louise's signal to meet was two waves of the left hand.
9. Miss Williams was critical of Tommy's valentine because he did not sign his full name.
10. Marguerite and Louise taught each other the Tut language.

***Suggested Essay Topics***

1. Describe Marguerite's new friend. What were Marguerite's feelings toward the friend? Do you think the description is an accurate one? Explain.
2. Describe Tommy Valdon and his actions? What were Marguerite's reactions to Tommy in public? Do you think these actions are typical of her actual feelings? Explain.

# Chapter 21

New Characters:

**Joyce:** *Bailey's first love outside the family*

**Mrs. Goodman:** *a customer in the Store who gives the reader information about the whereabouts of Joyce*

***Summary***

Chapter 21 describes the sexual experiments of Bailey. While Marguerite serves as the lookout, Bailey takes girls into a tent he constructed in the back yard. Bailey finally has sexual relations with Joyce, a new girl in the community. Marguerite explains that Joyce was Bailey's first love outside the family.

Mrs. Goodman, at the end of the chapter, tells Momma that Joyce has left Stamps with one of those railroad porters. Bailey is at first despondent, but he is finally able to summarize the situation by saying, "She's got someone to do it to her all the time now."

***Analysis***

The theme of maturation is again very evident in Chapter 21; it seems, however, that it is more Bailey than Marguerite who is physically maturing. Bailey is struggling to gain sexual knowledge from the local girls. He finally develops a sexual relationship with Joyce, the newcomer to Stamps.

Imagery helps the reader visualize the new character Joyce. For example, Marguerite says that Joyce walked "as if she were carrying a load of wood." Dialect is evident; for example, when Mrs. Goodman tells what has happened to Joyce, Momma says, "Do, Lord." The simile is used to describe Bailey's initial reaction to Joyce's leaving; Marguerite says, "He closed in upon himself like a pond swallowing a stone." Mrs. Henderson uses a metaphor to describe Marguerite as Marguerite eavesdrops; Mrs. Henderson says, "the Lord don't like little jugs with big ears."

Marguerite is the innocent in this chapter; she says, "I thought he would go to the hospital if he let her do that to him, so I warned him, 'Bailey, if you let her do that to you, you'll be sorry.'"

Marguerite is resentful of Joyce—at first because of her relationship with Bailey and later because of her leaving him. "If I had disliked Joyce while she had Bailey in her grasp, I hated her for leaving." Bailey himself struggles to accept the fact. Marguerite describes how Bailey "lost interest in everything. He mulled around and it would be safe to say 'he paled.'"

Resolution comes at the end of the chapter when Bailey accepts his loss and he and Marguerite go on to other things—a sign of maturity.

***Study Questions***

1. What kind of shelter did Bailey build in the back yard?
2. What did he do there in the shelter?
3. What roles were assigned to Marguerite?
4. What was the signal that an adult was approaching?
5. The children were prohibited from going to the movies during a certain period each year. When was this time?

6. What actions did Bailey begin to exhibit away from Joyce as their love affair progressed?
7. Who was Bailey's first love outside the family?
8. How did the community see Joyce, as evidenced by Mrs. Goodman?
9. What happened to Joyce?
10. How did Bailey convince them all that he was sick?

### *Answers*

1. Bailey made a tent in the backyard.
2. In the shelter Bailey introduced girls to the mysteries of sex.
3. Marguerite was assigned the roles of lookout and baby.
4. Marguerite would lift the flap, and Bailey would know that an adult was approaching.
5. The children were not allowed to go to a movie during Passover Week.
6. As the love affair progressed, Bailey's stealing increased.
7. Bailey's first love was Joyce.
8. Mrs. Goodman said that Joyce was like her mother and was a loose girl.
9. She ran away with a railroad porter.
10. Bailey convinced them that he was sick when he did not fret over the molasses and sulphur.

### *Suggested Essay Topics*

1. Describe Joyce. How do you think Joyce really felt about Bailey? Explain your answer.
2. Describe Bailey's reactions to Joyce's leaving. Compare and contrast his reactions to the time that another terrible thing happened in his life: when Mr. Freeman raped Marguerite.

# Chapter 22

New Character:

**George Taylor:** *widower of Mrs. Florida Taylor and a visitor to the homes in the area*

### *Summary*

Chapter 22 describes the rainy night when Mr. Taylor appears unexpectedly at the door. Mr. Taylor had been taking meals all over town since the death of his wife. He begins to tell them about dreams of his deceased wife.

Marguerite listens to the tales and recalls her fear at Mrs. Taylor's funeral. When her grandmother asks her to go into the kitchen, Marguerite finds she is frightened of even going into the kitchen alone.

Marguerite lays a pallet for Mr. Taylor in Uncle Willie's room.

### *Analysis*

In this chapter, Angelou's vivid imagery helps us visualize Mrs. Taylor's funeral. The reader can see the "black-dressed usher" and smell the "sickening black clothes worn in summer weather." Marguerite finds the entire funeral difficult to bear, especially when she must view Mrs. Taylor in the coffin. This vivid depiction also enables the reader to learn more about funeral customs in Stamps.

### *Study Questions*

1. On what kind of night did Mr. Taylor come to visit?
2. What book did Marguerite plan to read on such a night?
3. Why would Willie encourage Marguerite to close the store early on such a night?
4. What room functioned also as a sitting room?
5. What kind of weather threatened a tornado?
6. What did Uncle Willie read at night?
7. What did the family eat that night?
8. What did Marguerite fear Mr. Taylor might do?

9. What did Mr. Taylor say that his wife was saying?
10. Where did Mr. Taylor sleep that night?

***Answers***

1. Mr. Taylor came on a stormy night.
2. Marguerite planned to read *Jane Eyre* on such a night.
3. Uncle Willie would encourage her to close early and save on electricity.
4. Mrs. Henderson's bedroom functioned as a sitting room.
5. The wind blew and the sky was clear; this threatened a tornado.
6. Uncle Willie read the *Almanac* at night.
7. The family ate soup, cornbread, and sweet potatoes.
8. Marguerite feared that Mr. Taylor might marry her grandmother.
9. Mr. Taylor said his wife was saying "Children."
10. Mr. Taylor slept on a pallet in Uncle Willie's room.

***Suggested Essay Topics***

1. Describe Mr. Taylor as he is portrayed by Angelou.
2. Describe Mrs. Taylor's funeral as seen through Marguerite's eyes. What kind of experience is it for Marguerite.

# Chapter 23

New Characters:

**The principal of Lafayette County Training School**

**Mr. Edward Donleavy**: *a man running for election and the white speaker at the graduation ceremonies for Marguerite's class*

**Henry Reed**: *the valedictorian*

***Summary***

Chapter 23 describes the excitement of the community members who have friends and family in graduation ceremonies at Lafayette County Training School. Marguerite is particularly excited because this is her eighth-grade graduation.

During the ceremony Mr. Edward Donleavy, a white man who is running for election, comes on the stage. The white man who accompanies Mr. Donleavy to the stage actually takes the seat of the principal. Mr. Donleavy promises a paved playing field in exchange for their vote. He tells of the accomplishments of white schools in the area. After his speech Mr. Donleavy leaves the ceremony.

Sadness and shame fill the room. The participants feel that they have lost control of their ceremony and their lives. Henry Reed, the valedictorian, at last rallies the group; he leads them in "Lift Ev'ry Voice and Sing." As a result, "We were on top again."

***Analysis***

Mr. Donleavy seems to have certain preconceived notions about the group he is addressing. He sees them as sports figures and not scholars. The reward he offers in exchange for their vote—a paved playing field—is something the white schools already have. The festive mood of the crowd is taken away by the bricks of the graduation speaker.

The reader sees firsthand racial discrimination as the unknown white man goes to the stage and takes the seat of the principal. As the graduating class sings, Marguerite becomes "a proud member of the wonderful, beautiful Negro race."

Imagery helps the reader visualize the graduating class with their butter-yellow pique dresses. Foreshadowing, however, gives the reader an indication that all will not go well at the graduation; Marguerite says, "I was overcome with a presentiment of worse things to come."

Marguerite continues to mature in Chapter 23. She realizes that the boys have also "become more friendly, more outgoing." The fact of her graduation is an indication that Marguerite is no longer the child who arrives by train in Stamps after her parents' divorce.

### *Study Questions*

1. Why were the graduates coming to school without books, tablets, and pencils?
2. What was the name of the school from which Marguerite was graduating?
3. How many buildings composed the training school?
4. How old was Marguerite at this graduation?
5. From what grade was Marguerite graduating? What was the year of her graduation?
6. Why do you think Mr. Donleavy came to the graduation ceremony?
7. Even though Marguerite's last name began with a "J," she would be one of the first called at the graduation ceremonies. Why?
8. The unknown white man who came on stage took a seat which did not belong to him. Whose seat did he take?
9. For what did the speaker praise the graduates of the training school?
10. Who led the singing and made the graduates proud?

### *Answers*

1. The graduates were thinking of the future; they were coming to school without supplies, like travelers without a destination in mind.

2. The school was called Lafayette County Training School.
3. It had two buildings: main classrooms and the grade school and home economics building.
4. Marguerite was 12 at this graduation.
5. Marguerite was graduating from the eighth grade in 1940.
6. Mr. Donleavy came to the ceremony to try to secure the vote of the community.
7. Marguerite would be one of the first called because of her work.
8. The white man took the principal's seat.
9. The speaker praised the graduates who had done well in sports.
10. The valedictorian, Henry Reed, led the group in singing.

***Suggested Essay Topics***

1. Compare and contrast the plans for the fall for Central School and Lafayette County Training School. Do you think that the parents will vote for Mr. Donleavy? Explain your answer.
2. How were the graduates made to feel unimportant? How were the graduates made to feel important again? Do you think that the unimportant feeling will occur again for the graduates? Explain.

# Chapter 24

New Characters:

**The nurse of Dentist Lincoln:** *described by Mrs. Henderson as "snippity"*

**Dr. Lincoln:** *a dentist in Stamps*

**Dr. Baker:** *a dentist in Texarkana, Arkansas*

### *Summary*

Chapter 24 describes in detail the pain that Marguerite experiences with her tooth and the prejudice she experiences at the office of Dr. Lincoln. After Marguerite and Mrs. Henderson wait over an hour in the sun, Dr. Lincoln refuses to see Marguerite. He says, "I'd rather stick my hand in a dog's mouth than in a nigger's." After Mrs. Henderson "backed up inside herself for a few minutes," Mrs. Henderson walks inside the office without knocking. Later Marguerite and her grandmother make a trip all the way to Texarkana, Arkansas, to get help for the tooth.

Mrs. Henderson later tells Uncle Willie what happened when she went inside the office again. She asked Dr. Lincoln for the money he owed her. Dr. Lincoln explained that he had repaid the money some time ago, but Mrs. Henderson insisted that there was now interest; she took ten dollars for the trip to Texarkana as full payment. "Even though by rights he was paid up before, I figger, he gonna be that kind of nasty, he gonna have to pay for it."

Marguerite, however, prefers her fanciful version of what happened inside the office when Mrs. Henderson returned. Marguerite's version includes her grandmother's growing to a height of 10 feet, turning the nurse into a "crocus sack of chickenfeed," and evicting the dentist from the town.

### *Analysis*

Marguerite states that the pain was so bad that she prayed "to have the building collapse on her left jaw." Unfortunately, Dr. Lincoln, the white dentist in Stamps, states that he will not "treat nigra."

Angelou helps the reader visualize the aching teeth: "two cavities that were rotten to the gums." "Her eyes were blazing like live coals" for the pain. She makes use of personification when she calls the cavity the "Angel of the candy counter" and in the clause "pieces of sanity pushed themselves forward."

The theme of maturation takes a back seat in Chapter 24; it is the theme of social realism that is prominent. The reader sees firsthand the racism and segregation in Stamps as the white dentist refuses to "treat nigra, colored people." His unkind words cut Marguerite to the quick, but her grandmother finds retribution in her own way.

***Study Questions***

1. Who did Marguerite, in her imagination, think brought her pain?
2. What food brought the pain to Marguerite?
3. What remedies did Marguerite think of to take care of the pain?
4. Who was the dentist in Stamps?
5. Where was the "nearest Negro dentist"?
6. What was the name of the Texarkana dentist that Marguerite would visit?
7. Where did they get the money to go out of town?
8. How did they get to Texarkana?
9. Why was Marguerite not afraid of the dentist in Texarkana?
10. Why did Dr. Lincoln give Mrs. Henderson the $10?

***Answers***

1. The Angel of the candy counter brought the pain to Marguerite.
2. The pain was brought by the stolen Milky Ways, Mounds, Mr. Goodbars and Hersheys with Almonds.
3. Marguerite thought of having a building fall on her left jaw or jumping in the well.
4. The dentist in Stamps was Dr. Lincoln.
5. The "nearest Negro dentist" was in Texarkana.
6. Marguerite was going to Dr. Baker in Texarkana.
7. Marguerite and Mrs. Henderson got $10 from Dr. Lincoln.
8. They took the Greyhound to Texarkana.
9. Marguerite was not afraid of the dentist because her grandmother was there.

10. Mrs. Henderson confronted the dentist directly. She reminded him of the time she loaned him money. She told him there would now be interest on the money. The dentist paid her the $10 to get rid of her after she shamed him. He required her to sign a receipt so that the issue would never come up again.

### *Suggested Essay Topics*

1. Why did the dentist not treat Marguerite? Describe the humiliation he heaped on Mrs. Henderson and her granddaughter.
2. How did Mrs. Henderson seek retribution from the white dentist? Were her actions a surprise to the reader? Explain.

# Chapter 25

New Characters:

**Mr. Bubba:** *a Black man*

**Nameless white man:** *man who taunts Bailey*

### *Summary*

Chapter 25 describes in detail how Bailey sees a "colorless" person pulled from the river; Bailey is forced to help carry the body and is threatened with being locked in the calaboose. Bailey is horrified at what he has seen. It is at this time that Mrs. Henderson decides that they are going on a trip to California.

### *Analysis*

Bailey is maturing and as a young, virile male is a threat to the caste system in the eyes of many white men; in this chapter one white male reminds him of "his place."

The event profoundly affects Bailey. He tries to tell his family what he has seen and Marguerite notes that he talks so fast that he forgets to stutter. Marguerite tells the reader that Bailey's "little face was no longer black but a dirty, colorless gray" after he sees the dead man.

Imagery helps the reader visualize what Bailey saw: "he had no color at all. He was bloated like a ball." A simile gives additional information on the dead body; for example, Bailey says that the dead man was "all rolled up like a mummy" Marguerite uses personification to describe Bailey's reactions to the sights he saw. For example, "his soul just crawled behind his heart"; this was Bailey's way of coping.

Bailey is beginning to try to unravel the "enigma that young Southern Black boys start to unravel." Marguerite also is maturing. She is beginning to understand her grandmother and is able to stand apart and observe what is going on in her life. Mrs. Henderson tells the children "that we were growing up, that we needed to be with our parents, that Uncle Willie was, after all, crippled, that she was getting old." These are all indications that Marguerite is maturing.

The reader again sees firsthand the horrors of discrimination and racial violence in the 1940s in Stamps as Bailey watches the "colorless" body drawn from the water.

***Study Questions***

1. What is the saying among Black Americans which describes Momma's secretiveness?
2. What plan did Momma make when Bailey came home with his story of the body?
3. Where did Mrs. Henderson get the material to make Marguerite's new clothes?
4. What did Bailey do with the body?
5. How did Uncle Willie respond to Bailey's story?
6. How did Momma respond to Bailey's story?
7. Why did Marguerite think that they were going to California?
8. What two promises did Marguerite make to Bailey?
9. How did they get the transportation to California?
10. Who would go to California first?

***Answers***

1. "If you ask a Negro where he's been, he'll tell you where he's going."
2. Mrs. Henderson began to plan to take the children to California.
3. Mrs. Henderson got the material for the clothes for Marguerite from the trunks of neighbors who had the material packed away for a long time.
4. Bailey helped carry the body in the calaboose.
5. Uncle Willie responded that he did not know "what the world was coming to."
6. Momma prayed. Her prayer this time was, "God rest his soul, poor man.
7. Marguerite thought the finding of the body was the real reason for the trip to California. She thought their grandmother was getting them away from a volatile situation.
8. One promise was that she would not allow him to be buried without making sure that he was dead and the other was that Marguerite would not disturb Bailey when "his soul was sleeping."
9. Momma traded groceries for a pass on the railroad.
10. Momma and Marguerite would go to California first. Bailey would follow later.

***Suggested Essay Topics***

1. Why did Momma say that she is going to take the children to California? Why did Marguerite think Mrs. Henderson is going to do this? Why do you think that there exists this discrepancy?
2. Marguerite indicates that her grandmother is secretive. Why does the text indicate that this is so? Can you think of other reasons for this? Explain your answer.

# Chapter 26

New Character:

**Daddy Clidell:** *a successful businessman who moves the family to San Francisco and becomes Marguerite's stepfather*

### *Summary*

Chapter 26 describes Momma and Marguerite's trip to and arrival in California. The chapter tells of the reunion of Vivian with her children and of the reunion of Grandmother Baxter with the children after their trip to San Francisco. The chapter also tells the story of Vivian Baxter's shooting her business partner. It was while they were in California that World War II began and Mother married Daddy Clidell.

### *Analysis*

Vivian Baxter openly confronts and shoots her business partner because he has not been "shouldering his portion of the responsibility" and because he curses her. The violence and conflict that was a way of life in St. Louis have followed them to California.

Imagery helps the reader visualize the shooting: "he reached her and flung both arms around her neck, dragging her to the floor."

Marguerite develops her way of coping with the move to California, which she describes to her readers. Marguerite states that the "intensity with which young people live demands that they 'blank out' as often as possible. I didn't actually think about facing Mother until the last day of our journey."

The physical growth of Marguerite is evident when she says that her mother was "smaller than memory would have her." As the years pass Marguerite also shows maturity when she recognizes the adjustments her grandmother has made. She tells how the "old Southern Negro woman who had lived her life under the left breast of her community learned to deal with white landlords, Mexican neighbors and Negro strangers."

### *Study Questions*

1. How did Marguerite deal with facing Mother again?

2. Why did Marguerite feel uncomfortable about seeing her mother again?
3. Where did Marguerite sleep in the apartment?
4. Where did Mother go after getting Marguerite and Mrs. Henderson settled into an apartment?
5. What kind of friends did Mrs. Henderson make?
6. What did Mrs. Henderson do after Vivian Baxter made arrangements for the move to San Francisco?
7. How did Bailey, Vivian, and Marguerite get to San Francisco?
8. With whom did Marguerite sleep in Oakland?
9. Why did Vivian get Marguerite up in the middle of the night?
10. What was Vivian's occupation?

***Answers***

1. Marguerite coped with the change that was to come by not thinking about it.
2. Marguerite felt uncomfortable about seeing her mother again because she felt guilty about what happened with Mr. Freeman; she wondered if his name would be mentioned or if she should say something about the situation.
3. Marguerite slept on a sofa that miraculously changed into a bed at night.
4. Marguerite's mother went to San Francisco to arrange living accommodations for her enlarged family.
5. Mrs. Henderson made the same kind of friends that she had always made. She made friends with churchgoers who talked of the hereafter.
6. Mrs. Henderson returned to Stamps after Vivian made arrangements for the move to San Francisco.
7. Vivian drove them to San Francisco.
8. Marguerite slept with Grandmother Baxter in Oakland.
9. Vivian got Marguerite up in the middle of the night to have

a party for them with hot chocolate and biscuits and dancing by Vivian.

10. Vivian played pinochle for money or ran a poker game.

***Suggested Essay Topics***

1. Marguerite describes her mother when she first saw her in St. Louis. In this chapter she describes Mother when she first saw her in California. Compare and contrast the two descriptions.
2. Mother has a party for Bailey and Marguerite. Compare and contrast this party with a typical party. What does this party tell you about Vivian?

# Chapter 27

***Summary***

In this chapter, Marguerite describes the Fillmore district of San Francisco where the Asian population dwindles before her eyes and their shops "were taken over by enterprising Negro businessmen." Marguerite explains that as the Japanese are sent to camps, "the Negroes entered with their loud jukeboxes, their just-released animosities and the relief of escape from Southern bonds."

The chapter also tells the story of the white woman who would not sit beside the "Negro civilian on the streetcar." Her reason is that he is "a draft dodger who was a Negro as well," while her own son is fighting in Iwo Jima. His response is, "Then ask your son to look around for my arm, which I left over there."

***Analysis***

Prejudice and discrimination, Marguerite finds, exist in California just as they do in Stamps. Marguerite notes the Japanese disappearing and Negroes entering after World War II. She reflects that many people might have expected "Negro newcomers" to show sympathy and support for the "dislodged Japanese." This did not happen, in her way of thinking, because " . . . the sensations of common relationship were misssing." She describes, using personification, how "Pride and Prejudice stalked in tandem the beautiful hills." Person-against-society conflict occurs as Marguerite struggles to adapt to a new society and new people.

Angelou continues to use many stylistic devices. Imagery helps the reader visualize the " . . . naval officers with their well-dressed wives and clean white babies" and the "well-kept old women in chauffeured cars and blond girls in buckskin shoes and cashmere sweaters. . . . " She uses metaphor and simile in her descriptions of San Francisco; for example, San Francisco is known to its residents as "the Bay, the fog, Sir Francis Drake Hotel, Top o' the Mark, Chinatown, the Sunset District and so on . . . "

In Chapter 27 Marguerite reminds the reader that she is 13 years old and at last has a sense of belonging. She is beginning to set goals for herself:

> . . . The city became for me the ideal of what I wanted to be as a grownup. Friendly but never gushing, cool but not frigid or distant, distinguished without the awful stiffness.

***Study Questions***

1. Where did Marguerite reside in San Francisco?
2. Which population dwindled in number in San Francisco?
3. Who took over the Japanese shops?
4. Which area became San Francisco's Harlem?
5. Who recruited the Black newcomers?
6. In what city did Marguerite first feel a sense of belonging?
7. Where had the blacks experienced concentration camp living?
8. To what creature did Marguerite compare San Francisco?
9. Why did the white matron refuse to sit by the civilian on the streetcar?
10. What did the civilian ask the white matron's son to find for him in Iwo Jima?

***Answers***

1. Marguerite resided in "San Francisco's Fillmore district, or the Western addition. . . . "
2. Marguerite says that the " . . . Asian population dwindled before my eyes. . . . " Many of the Japanese left for what amounted to enforced internment in camps much like concentration camps.
3. Marguerite stated that "enterprising Negro businessmen" took over the businesses.
4. The Japanese area became San Francisco's Harlem.
5. The war-plant labor scouts recruited the Black newcomers.
6. Marguerite first felt a sense of belonging in the city of San Francisco.
7. Blacks had experienced concentration-camp living in sharecroppers' cabins.
8. Marguerite compared San Francisco to a woman.
9. The white matron refused to sit by the civilian because he was a Negro and a draft dodger.
10. The civilian asked the matron's son to find his arm for him in Iwo Jima.

***Suggested Essay Topics***

1. Compare and contrast San Francisco with Stamps.
2. Why was the "Black newcomer" indifferent to the Japanese removal? Would you say that there is less prejudice in San Francisco than in Stamps? Explain your answer.

# Chapter 28

New Character:

**Miss Kirwin:** *Marguerite's teacher in San Francisco*

***Summary***

Chapter 28 describes the education of Marguerite in the public schools and at the California Labor School. She describes the public schools as often violent; fights were commonplace.

Marguerite receives a scholarship to the California Labor School. Marguerite has one good experience there; she develops a new allegiance in her life: Miss Kirwin and her information. This teacher brings her knowledge to Marguerite and makes an impression on Marguerite for the rest of her life. Years later Marguerite finds the school is on the "House Un-American Activities list of subversive organizations."

***Analysis***

The setting and characters in California are important parts of Chapter 28. The reader experiences firsthand the social groups in the high school near Marguerite's home and at George Washington High School and the teachers at the California Labor School.

Marguerite attends the high school near her home and is thrown into a group of "young ladies . . . faster, brasher, meaner and more prejudiced than any I had met at Lafayette County Training School." Negro and Mexican students carry knives to the public school to use on the white girls with "no shield of fearlessness." The conflict for Marguerite is somewhat resolved when she goes to the California Labor School.

Angelou helps the reader visualize Miss Kirwin, "who was a tall, florid, buxom lady with battleship-gray hair." She also uses dialect to tell how the "Negro girls . . . claimed to have known the bright lights of Big D (Dallas) or T Town (Tulsa, Oklahoma)," and how Miss Kirwin always responded with "Correct" to any right answer.

Marguerite is now 14. She is given a scholarship to the California Labor School, where she learns to move like her teacher and "occupy space." The reader finds Marguerite trying to assess herself realistically. She describes the dance lessons she takes to change her body and her feelings about herself. She hopes the lessons will "make my legs big and widen my hips."

***Study Questions***

1. Describe the girls in the high school near Marguerite's home in San Francisco.
2. Where was "T Town"?
3. What did the girls carry in their pompadours?
4. Whom did these brash girls intimidate?
5. What was the name of the first real school that Marguerite attended?
6. How well did Marguerite measure up to the other students at the first real school she attended?
7. Who was Marguerite's favorite teacher there?
8. Where did Marguerite go on a scholarship?
9. What two classes did she take in the evening?
10. What made the California Labor School a questionable school in the eyes of some people?

***Answers***

1. The girls in the high school near Marguerite's home were "faster, brasher, meaner, and more prejudiced than any I met at Lafayette County Training School."
2. The students called Tulsa, Oklahoma, "T Town."
3. Some of the "Negro girls . . . put knives in their tall pompadours. . . . "
4. Some of the "Negro girls . . . intimidated the white girls and those Black and Mexican students who had no shield of fearlessness."
5. The name of the first real school that Marguerite attended was George Washington High School.

6. Marguerite was put up two semesters on her arrival, but she was not the most brilliant student there.
7. Marguerite's favorite teacher was Miss Kirwin.
8. Marguerite attended the California Labor School on a scholarship.
9. In the evenings Marguerite attended dance and drama classes.
10. The school was a questionable school because it was on the "House Un-American Activities list of subversive organizations."

***Suggested Essay Topics***

1. Compare and contrast the California Labor School and Marguerite's experience there with the California public schools and Marguerite's experience there.
2. Marguerite learned much from Mrs. Flowers and Mrs. Kirwin. Compare and contrast these two women in Marguerite's life.

# Chapter 29

New Character:

**Red Leg:** *a member of the Black underground and a visitor to the Clidell home*

***Summary***

This chapter describes the new life with Mother and Daddy Clidell. The boarders in Daddy Clidell's house are presented briefly to the reader as characters who do not speak. Daddy Clidell is exposed to the reader in more detail in this chapter. Through Marguerite's description Clidell Jackson emerges as a real person who brings the Black underground into the big house. Mr. Red Leg, a member of the Black underground, is one visitor to the home who is very kind to Marguerite. Marguerite relates a story he tells her about outwitting a white man.

### *Analysis*

The prejudice that is obvious in Chapter 29 is that of Blacks against whites. Marguerite hears many stories from the Black underground. In the tales, "the Black man . . . won out every time over the powerful, arrogant white." The individual characters themselves are symbols of the entire Black underground and the white race; the triumph of a Black character over a greedy white person is symbolic of the underground's longed-for triumph over their white oppressors.

When Marguerite learns of Vivian's relationship with Mr. Clidell, she prepares herself to "accept Daddy Clidell as one more faceless name added to Mother's roster of conquests." She finds, however, that "his character beckoned and elicited admiration."

A maturing Marguerite helps the reader to meet a part of society in San Francisco that one might never meet again: the Black underground of the 1940s in San Francisco. Through the stories of Mr. Red Leg in the 1940s the reader senses the California caste system which pits Blacks against whites.

### *Study Questions*

1. How many rooms were in the house in which Marguerite lives in San Francisco?
2. Who was Uncle Jim's wife?
3. How long had Daddy Clidell been to school?
4. What did Daddy Clidell teach Marguerite while her mother taught them manners, hygiene, and posture?
5. What comment did people make when Mother, Daddy Clidell, and Marguerite were seen together?
6. Who were three of the members of the Black underground that Marguerite met?
7. What is a "mark"?
8. Why were the tales all satisfying to Marguerite?
9. What did all the marks have in common?
10. What belief appeals to one who is unable to compete legally with his fellow citizens?

***Answers***

1. The house had 14 rooms.
2. Uncle Jim's wife was Aunt Boy.
3. Daddy Clidell had been to school only three years.
4. Daddy Clidell taught Marguerite to play cards.
5. People commented that Marguerite looked like Daddy Clidell.
6. Members of the underground included Stonewall Jimmy, Just Black, Cool Clyde, Tight Coat and Red Leg.
7. A "mark" is a victim.
8. The tales were satisfying to Marguerite because the Black man won every time.
9. The marks all wanted something for nothing.
10. The belief that it is all right to do a little robbing appeals to one who is unable to compete legally.

***Suggested Essay Topics***

1. Describe the diverse boarders and the visitors to the household where Marguerite lives. Are there ways that these boarders might be alike? Explain.
2. Discuss the prejudices and discrimination described in Chapter 29. Compare this prejudice and discrimination with that Marguerite experienced in Stamps.

# Chapter 30

New Character:

**Dolores Stockland:** *Daddy's new girlfriend*

***Summary***

Chapter 30 takes place in San Francisco, Southern California where Marguerite's father now lives, Mexico, and then in Southern

California again. At her father's invitation Marguerite leaves San Francisco and her mother to visit her father in southern California. There Marguerite meets Dolores, her father's new girlfriend, for the first time. Marguerite and Dolores's relationship is a strained one from the first meeting. Dolores is surprised to find Bailey's daughter is almost as old as she; Marguerite is surprised that her father's girlfriend is very young. The two young women find their habits are very different and that living under one roof makes for problems.

One day Bailey, Sr., takes Marguerite with him to Mexico for a night of drinking and carousing. Because her father is intoxicated, Marguerite, who has never driven before, ends up having to drive home and wrecks the car. Bailey gets her out of the difficulty, but the incident causes hard feelings between father and daughter.

***Analysis***

Marguerite feels very resentful toward her father. She does not think he recognizes her accomplishment in driving and she questions how he was able to recover so quickly from his drunkenness. In addition, conflict has existed between Dolores and Marguerite since the first time that they meet. Marguerite fails to be the child that Dolores prepares to meet and Dolores is much younger and much more "tight" than Marguerite would have preferred. Marguerite believes that Dolores is attempting to pose as "the Black bourgeoisie without the material basis to support the poses." She sees Dolores as trying to be something she is not. Dolores, on the other hand, sees Marguerite not as a child but as a rival.

***Study Questions***

1. Why did Marguerite leave San Francisco?
2. Where did she go?
3. Why did Marguerite not find Dolores at first?
4. Why did Dolores not recognize Marguerite at first?
5. What did Bailey give as an excuse for going to Mexico?
6. Why was Marguerite's father such a good cook?

7. Why did Dolores not speak Spanish, according to Marguerite?
8. What was Marguerite's daddy's specialty?
9. What did the border guard on the way into Mexico say he would do with Marguerite?
10. Why was Marguerite's father impressive to the Mexican peasants in the cantina?

### *Answers*

1. Marguerite left San Francisco to visit with her father.
2. Bailey, Sr., lived in Southern California.
3. At first Marguerite did not find Dolores because Dolores was in her early 20s and much younger than Marguerite expected.
4. Dolores did not find Marguerite at first because Marguerite was older than Dolores had expected; Bailey, Sr., had told Dolores that his children were eight and nine. Marguerite also believed that she was uglier than Dolores had expected.
5. Bailey said that they were going to Mexico to buy food for the weekend.
6. He was such a good cook because he worked in the kitchen of a naval hospital, had been in France during World War I, and had worked as a doorman at the exclusive Breakers Hotel.
7. Dolores did not speak Spanish because "her mouth was too taut and her tongue was too still to attempt the strange sounds," according to Marguerite.
8. Marguerite's father's specialty was Mexican food.
9. The border guard they met on their way into Mexico said he would marry Marguerite and have many children.
10. Marguerite's father impressed the Mexicans in the cantina because he was American, was Black, spoke Spanish fluently, had money, could drink tequila with the best of them, was

liked by the women, and was tall and handsome and generous.

***Suggested Essay Topics***

1. Compare and contrast Marguerite's feelings toward her father after the trip to Mexico and the feelings she had toward him before the trip.
2. Describe the residence of Dolores and Bailey, Sr. How does the residence reflect the personality of Bailey, Sr.? How does it reflect the personality of Dolores?

# Chapter 31

**Summary**

In this chapter, Angelou describes the quarrel between Dolores and Marguerite's father which occurs after Bailey, Sr., and Marguerite return home from Mexico. When the angry father leaves the trailer to visit neighbors, Marguerite feels sorry for Dolores and tries to make up with her. Dolores will not make up and calls Vivian a whore; Marguerite slaps Dolores. During the scuffle that follows, Dolores cuts Marguerite.

When Dolores goes after her with a hammer, Marguerite locks herself in the car. The neighbors, including Marguerite's father, hear the disturbance and take Dolores inside the trailer to quiet her. Marguerite longs to go inside to show her father her wound, but she is reluctant to be seen with blood on her clothes because of her "feminine training." When Bailey, Sr., sits down in the car with Marguerite, he sees the blood and takes her to a neighbor's for treatment and for shelter.

The next morning Marguerite considers running away. She prepares some food to take with her. When the neighbor's door closes and locks behind her, Marguerite realizes she cannot go back.

### *Analysis*

Bailey, Sr., often leaves Dolores at home and goes to Mexico to drink, "go off with his women," and have a good time. Dolores is left alone to fume while he is away. Dolores and Marguerite have had problems from the beginning, but in this chapter the two engage in verbal and physical conflict. As a result of the violent physical confrontation, Marguerite is severely cut.

The development and growth of Marguerite are quite evident as a major theme in Chapter 31. Marguerite, who is seen as a rival by her father's girlfriend, now takes the initiative to make her own decisions, to strike out on her own, and even to say, "At fifteen life had taught me undeniably that surrender, in its place, was as honorable as resistance, especially if one had no choice."

### *Study Questions*

1. What was Dolores doing when Marguerite and her father returned from Mexico?
2. Why did Dolores say she was angry with Bailey, Sr.?
3. How did Marguerite feel about her father after he quarreled with Dolores?
4. Why did Marguerite feel guilty when her father left?
5. Marguerite tried to make up with Dolores. How did she see herself as she went about this task?
6. Why did Marguerite become so enraged at the thought that her mother was a whore?
7. Why did her father not take her to a hospital?
8. Why did Marguerite decide to leave the trailer?
9. What did Marguerite take with her when she ran away?
10. Why did Marguerite not change her mind about leaving?

### *Answers*

1. Dolores was making curtains when Marguerite and her father returned from their trip.

2. Dolores said she was angry with Bailey, Sr., because he let his children come between them.
3. Marguerite thought her father was mean for quarreling with Dolores after he had enjoyed his trip and was unable to be kind to the woman who had waited for him.
4. Marguerite felt sorry and guilty because she had enjoyed herself also.
5. As Marguerite tried to make up with Dolores, she saw herself as merciful, good, favorable, Christian, and just.
6. Marguerite becomes furious when Dolores calls Marguerite's mother a whore. This accusation arouses doubts in Marguerite's mind. Marguerite became enraged because she could not live with her mother if the charge were true and she desperately wanted to do so.
7. He did not take her to a hospital because of the scandal that would result when others found out that Bailey Johnson's daughter had been cut by his lady friend.
8. Marguerite decided to leave the trailer because she could not bear the contempt or pity of the occupants of the trailer, because her father and Dolores would be relieved, and because she did not see suicide as an option.
9. Marguerite took tuna sandwiches, Band-Aids, and some money with her when she walked out.
10. Marguerite did not change her mind about leaving because the door to the trailer locked when she closed it.

***Suggested Essay Topics***

1. Discuss the sources of conflict between Dolores and Marguerite. What were the results of this conflict?
2. Why do you think that Marguerite did not return home to her mother immediately after the fight?

# Chapter 32

New Characters:

**Bootsie:** *the acknowledged leader of the junkyard gang*

**Lee Arthur:** *the only boy who ran with the junkyard gang and lived at home*

**Juan:** *the gang member who gives Marguerite a black lace handkerchief*

### *Summary*

After she runs away from the neighbor's home, Marguerite finds an abandoned car in which she sleeps that night. The next morning when she awakes, she sees a group of young faces peering in at her. The faces are those of a gang of young people who live in the junked cars. Marguerite lives with the gang for one month.

The month is not a bad one. Marguerite learns to drive, dance, and curse. In addition, she learns tolerance and develops some security.

At the end of the month she calls her mother and asks for fare home. Before she leaves she receives two gifts: a black lace handkerchief from Juan and a friendship ring from a girl in the gang. After she flies to her mother, Marguerite says, "I was at home, again."

### *Analysis*

The reader sees a great deal of growth in Marguerite in this chapter: "After a month my thinking processes had so changed that I was hardly recognizable to myself."; "During the month that I spent in the yard I learned to drive . . . to curse and to dance"; and "The unquestioning acceptance by my peers had dislodged the familiar insecurity."

Another motif which emerges in this chapter is that of education. The junkyard has become the school facility and the gang members the teachers. Marguerite is the first to acknowledge all the learning she receives from this group:

> After a month my thinking processes
> had so changed that I was hardly recognizable
> to myself. The unquestioning acceptance by
> my peers had dislodged the familiar insecurity...
> I was never again to sense myself so solidly
> outside the pale of the human race. The lack of
> criticism evidenced by our ad hoc community
> influenced me, and set a tone of tolerance
> for my life.

Character-against-society conflict is also a theme in Chapter 32. Marguerite joins a group of youth who live in a junkyard. They live in an orderly fashion and set their own rules: no two people of opposite sex can sleep together, no one can steal, everyone must work, and all money is to be used communally. The group separates itself from the society about it. While she is with this group, Marguerite is at last able to let go of the familiar insecurity that she brought with her to the junkyard and emerge as a different, more self-assured person.

***Study Questions***

1. Why did Marguerite not try the games of chance in the penny arcade?
2. Where did Marguerite go after she left the arcade?
3. What solution did Marguerite find for her lack of shelter?
4. What fear did Marguerite have in her new shelter?
5. What did Marguerite see upon waking up the next morning?
6. Who was the leader of the group of youth?
7. What was the rule of the group?
8. How long did Marguerite live in the group?
9. What two gifts did Marguerite receive when she decided to leave?
10. How was Lee Arthur different from the others in the group?

***Answers***

1. Marguerite did not play the games of chance because she would only win more chances and not money.
2. Marguerite went to the library after she left the arcade.
3. Marguerite found a car in a junkyard in which to sleep.
4. Marguerite feared that rats might enter the car.
5. Marguerite saw faces peering in at her the next morning.
6. Bootsie was the leader of the group.
7. The rule was that no two people of opposite sex could sleep together.
8. Marguerite lived one month in the group.
9. Marguerite received a friendship ring and a black lace handkerchief.
10. Lee Arthur was the only one of the group who lived at home.

***Suggested Essay Topics***

1. Marguerite learns many important things in this chapter. Describe Marguerite's lessons learned with the group in the junkyard.
2. Describe the new social group to which Marguerite attached herself. By what standard did the group function successfully? In what ways did the group function unsuccessfully? Explain your answer.

# Chapter 33

***Summary***

Chapter 33 describes Marguerite's return to her mother. Marguerite is relieved upon arriving there. There are fun times when Marguerite, Vivian, and Bailey attend recreational dances. Bailey and his mother, however, are not getting along. Marguerite says they are entangled in what she calls the Oedipal skein: a love/power struggle.

Finally one night, Bailey comes in late. When Mother Dear asks Bailey if it is eleven o'clock, Bailey tells her it is one. Mother Dear says there is only one man, Daddy Clidell, in the family. A quarrel ensues. Bailey leaves home and goes to live in a hotel. Marguerite visits him there. When they have said all they can say, Marguerite leaves him alone.

***Analysis***

The development and growth of Bailey and Marguerite are quite evident in Chapter 33. Marguerite recognizes that she is growing. "I reasoned that I had given up some youth for knowledge." She also recognizes the progress toward maturation of Bailey: "Bailey was much older too. Even years older than I had become." At another point Marguerite explains that "Bailey was sixteen, small for his age, bright for any and hopelessly in love with Mother Dear." Marguerite expresses her feelings toward maturation: " growing up was not the painless process one would have thought it to be." Bailey, too, expresses his feelings toward maturity. He says that there comes a "time in every man's life when he must push off from the wharf of safety into the sea of chance."

***Study Questions***

1. How had the relationship between Marguerite and Bailey changed?
2. In what area were Marguerite and Bailey closer?
3. Why could Marguerite dance better now?
4. Name some of the musicians to whom Marguerite danced.
5. Name some of the dances Marguerite danced.
6. Why did Marguerite become less concerned with her mother's reputation, community image, and good name?
7. Whose side did Marguerite take in the battle between Bailey and Mother Dear?
8. Who were Mother Dear's friends?
9. Marguerite says that Bailey and Mother Dear were engaged

in a power/love struggle. What event finally led to Bailey's leaving the house?

10. What job did Bailey secure after leaving the house?

***Answers***

1. Bailey seems indifferent to Marguerite.
2. Marguerite and Bailey are closer in one area: dancing.
3. Marguerite's new assurance allows her to give herself up to the rhythms.
4. Marguerite dances to Count Basie, Cab Calloway, and Duke Ellington.
5. Marguerite dances the jitterbug, the Lindy, the Big Apple, and the Half Time Texas Hop.
6. Marguerite becomes less concerned with everything.
7. Marguerite is neutral in the battles between Bailey and Mother Dear.
8. Mother Dear's friends are her heroes and her friends are big men in rackets.
9. Bailey's coming in late is the event which led to his leaving the house.
10. Bailey, with Mother's help, secures a job on the Southern Pacific after leaving the house.

***Suggested Essay Topics***

1. What evidence does the reader have that Bailey is trying to grow up in this chapter?
2. Compare and contrast Bailey's friends with Mother Dear's friends.

# Chapter 34

New Characters:

**A receptionist:** *works at the employment office of the Market Street Railway Company in San Francisco*

**A street car conductorette:** *treats Marguerite with less than courtesy*

### *Summary*

This chapter describes in detail 15-year-old Marguerite's search for a job when her room begins to be as cheerful as a dungeon. She rules out many jobs and finally settles on streetcar conductorette. Vivian tells her that "They don't accept colored people on streetcars," but she encourages Marguerite to try for the job if she wants it. Even after a rebuke from the receptionist, Marguerite does not give up; she continues to apply and calls on Negro organizations to help. Marguerite at last is hired—just why she never knows. Marguerite becomes the first Negro conductorette on the San Francisco streetcars.

Marguerite returns to school after one semester and begins to cut classes. She and her mother agree to be honest with each other: Marguerite will tell her mother when she plans to cut classes. Marguerite may cut classes if her school work is up to standard and if she has no tests scheduled. Vivian explains that she does not want a white woman to tell her about her own daughter nor does she want to be placed in the position of lying to a white woman because Marguerite was not "woman enough to speak up."

Angelou states that the American Negro female adult is usually a formidable character; Angelou says this "is the inevitable outcome of the struggle won by survivors and deserves respect if not enthusiastic acceptance."

### *Analysis*

Marguerite pits herself against the social system when she goes after the job of streetcar conductorette—a job reserved for whites. She confronts the receptionist, uses every resource she knows, and is eventually given forms to complete—and a job. Marguerite

struggles to forgive the clerk and comes to accept her as a fellow victim. Marguerite herself recognizes that in her short life she has experienced "masculine prejudice, white illogical hate and Black lack of power."

Marguerite states that she

. . . as so much wiser and older, so much more independent, with a bank account and clothes that I had bought for myself, that I was sure that I had learned and earned the magic formula which would make me a part of the gay life my contemporaries led."

Later Marguerite says that "Without willing it, I had gone from being ignorant of being ignorant to being aware of being aware."

***Study Questions***

1. What did Marguerite think of her room after Bailey left?
2. Why did Marguerite not run away?
3. What did Marguerite decide to do instead of staying in her room or running away?
4. How old did one have to be to work at a defense job?
5. What did Mother say when she found out Marguerite wanted to work on the streetcars?
6. What did it mean when Mother said, "Can't do is like Don't Care"?
7. What were the offices of the Market Street Railway Company like?
8. Why did the receptionist first say that Marguerite could not be seen?
9. Did Marguerite forgive the receptionist?
10. What three forces did Marguerite face?

***Answers***

1. Marguerite thought her room had all the cheeriness of a dungeon after Bailey left.

2. Marguerite did not run away because it would be anticlimactic after Mexico and dull after the car lot.
3. Marguerite decided to get a job.
4. One had to be 15 to get a defense job.
5. Mother said that they did not "accept colored people on streetcars."
6. It meant that there was nothing one could not do and there should not be anything one did not care about.
7. The offices were dingy inside and drab in decor.
8. The receptionist first said Marguerite could not be seen because she was not sent by an agency.
9. Marguerite forgave the receptionist; she accepted her as a victim.
10. Marguerite faced masculine prejudice, white illogical hate, and Black lack of power.

***Suggested Essay Topics***

1. Discuss Marguerite's reactions to finding out from her mother that she could not be a worker on the streetcar. Would this be a typical reaction for a young girl at this time?
2. What discrimination did Marguerite say she had felt by the time she was 15? Do you think she would have felt the same types of discrimination if she were growing up today? Explain why you answered as you did.

# Chapter 35

New Character:

**Young man from down the street:** *the nameless father of Marguerite's child*

***Summary***

Chapter 35 describes in detail Marguerite's difficulty in accepting her sexuality. She reads a book on lesbianism and confuses the term *lesbianism* with *hermaphrodite.* She looks at her large hands and feet and at her undeveloped breasts and becomes convinced that she is a lesbian. She notes the development of some folds of skin and approaches her mother with her concerns. Her mother reassures her with the help of a dictionary.

When Marguerite sees an acquaintance undressing, she again has doubts about her femininity; she mistakes the "esthetic sense of beauty and the pure emotion of envy" for homosexuality. She wants "to be a woman, but that seemed to be a world to which I was to be eternally refused entrance."

At last to assure herself that she is normal, Marguerite asks a handsome boy up the street if he would like to have "a sexual intercourse" with her. The result of this one-time affair is Marguerite's pregnancy.

### *Analysis*

Even surrounding the sex act there is misunderstanding and conflict—not reassurance and understanding. Marguerite's friend "thought I was giving him something, and the fact of the matter was that it was my intention to take something from him." After the brief encounter, Marguerite's main concern is how to get home quickly. "He may have sensed that he had been used."

Angelou continues to employ many stylistic devices. For example, the simile in "my armpits were as smooth as my face" helps the reader visualize what the author is trying to convey. Marguerite uses the euphemism "pocketbook" for "vagina"; her mother tells her to use the clinical description, not "the Southern term."

The primary theme in Chapter 35 is maturation; Marguerite is becoming an adult and is facing many doubts and questions. Perhaps the fact that she has no close friend in California makes her plight seem more extraordinary to her. There is no resolution to her questions since at the end of the chapter she finds that she is to become a mother. The reader sees firsthand the problems of adolescence in American society in the 1940s.

### *Study Questions*

1. What book in Chapter 35 influenced Marguerite?

2. Where did Marguerite buy her shoes?
3. What book did Marguerite's mother use as a sex manual?
4. What did her mother ask for that helped Marguerite know that her bodily problems were not serious?
5. What nickname did Marguerite's mother use for Marguerite?
6. Where had the dictionary come from?
7. Why did Marguerite decide to find a boyfriend?
8. Who did Marguerite ask to have sex with her?
9. What attitude did Marguerite have after the affair?
10. Was the affair something Marguerite enjoyed and something that made her know she was normal?

***Answers***

1. *The Well of Loneliness* was a book that influenced Marguerite.
2. Marguerite bought her shoes in the old lady's comfort section of the shoe store.
3. *Webster's Dictionary* was the book they used.
4. If the situation had been serious, Marguerite's mother would have asked for scotch and water, not a beer.
5. Mother called Marguerite "Ritie."
6. The dictionary had been a gift for Daddy Clidell from Mother.
7. Marguerite decided to find a boyfriend to find out if she was a normal female and because she was finding a newly awakening sexual appetite.
8. Marguerite asked a boy up the street to have sex with her.
9. Marguerite's attitude was that she would "understand it all better by and by."
10. The affair left her with questions about her normalcy and she did not enjoy it at all.

***Suggested Essay Topics***

1. Marguerite had many doubts about herself. Is this normal in adolescence or is this unique with Marguerite? Explain.
2. Marguerite has many misconceptions. What are some of these misconceptions? Explain each.

# Chapter 36

***Summary***

In Chapter 36 Marguerite describes her emotions upon realizing she is pregnant. She takes little pleasure in the fact at first and staggers under the weight of it. She writes to Bailey, who advises her not to tell her mother about the pregnancy and to continue school. Marguerite listens. She does not lie about her pregnancy, but she does not tell others. She finds that school takes on new magic for her. Bailey comes home about halfway through her pregnancy.

During Marguerite's sixth month, Vivian goes to Alaska to open a night club. Two days after her graduation, Marguerite leaves a note for Daddy Clidell in which she tells him about the baby. She spends the next two weeks buying clothes for the baby, visiting the doctor and enjoying the event.

Marguerite delivers a healthy boy, but she describes her fears of holding the child. When he is three weeks old, her mother places the infant in bed with her. Her mother awakes her later and shows her the infant asleep at her side.

***Analysis***

The continuing motif of maturation is again evident in this final chapter as Marguerite delivers her baby. She expresses her feelings for this accomplishment in this way: "No one had bought him for me. No one had helped me endure the sickly gray months. I had had help in the child's conception, but no one could deny that I had had an immaculate pregnancy."

Part of her difficulty is that Marguerite must hide her pregnancy from those around her. She has a desire to finish school and

knows that if her pregnancy is revealed, she will have to leave school. She is successful in managing to hide her condition and indeed receives her diploma.

Marguerite is clearly uneasy with herself after the birth of the baby; she does trust herself to care for her own infant. "Wasn't I famous for awkwardness? Suppose I let him slip, or put my fingers on that throbbing pulse on the top of his head?"

Through her mother, however, she learns she can care for her baby: "If you're for the right thing, then you do it without thinking."

***Study Questions***

1. How does Marguerite feel about the pregnancy in the very beginning?
2. Who does Marguerite blame for the pregnancy?
3. Who does she inform about the pregnancy?
4. Where is Bailey when Marguerite realizes she is pregnant?
5. Why does Bailey tell Marguerite not to tell her mother about the pregnancy?
6. What does Bailey bring home to Marguerite from South America?
7. How does Marguerite feel about school as she studies during her last year?
8. Where does Vivian go during the sixth month of Marguerite's pregnancy?
9. Why does Vivian go there?
10. What does Vivian call Marguerite at the end of the book?

***Answers***

1. In the beginning, she thought the pregnancy was a catastrophe.
2. Marguerite blames only herself.
3. She tells Bailey about her pregnancy.

4. Bailey is at sea with the merchant marines when Marguerite told him.
5. Bailey suggests that Marguerite not to tell her mother about the pregnancy because her mother would make her leave school.
6. Bailey brings Marguerite a bracelet, the book *Look Homeward, Angel,* and dirty jokes.
7. Marguerite finds school to be magic.
8. Vivian goes to Alaska during Marguerite's sixth month.
9. She goes there to open a night club.
10. Vivian calls Marguerite by the name "Maya" at the end of the book.

***Suggested Essay Topics***

1. During her pregnancy and after the birth of her child, Marguerite felt several emotions. Describe these emotions. Why do you think she felt them?
2. What evidence do you have that Marguerite is a mature young woman at the end of *I Know Why the Caged Bird Sings*?

## SECTION THREE

# *Sample Analytical Paper Topics*

The following paper topics are designed to test your understanding of the novel as a whole and to analyze important themes and literary devices. Following each question is a sample outline to help get you started.

***Topic #1***

Marguerite accomplished many things in the short time Angelou records for us. Which accomplishments do you think are most meaningful to her? Explain each and why it was important.

***Outline***

I. Thesis Statement: *Marguerite had many accomplishments in the 16 years recorded in* I Know Why the Caged Bird Sings. *Three of them are very important: securing a job as a conductorette, graduating from high school, and giving birth.*

II. Securing a job as conductorette

   A. Was "first Negro on the San Francisco streetcar"

   B. Had wanted job and had worked hard to get it

   C. Felt had gone against the "system" and won

   D. Had controlled her own fate

III. Graduating from high school

A. Had been in many different schools

B. Had a good record

C. Had managed to graduate when pregnant and keep it a secret

D. An achievement—especially for a Black girl at that time in history

IV. Giving birth to baby

A. Had kept it a secret

B. Had finished school

C. Referred to it as a virgin pregnancy

D. Later would say best thing that ever happened to her

***Topic #2***

Contrast Bailey Johnson, Sr.'s wife (Vivian Baxter Johnson) and his mistress Dolores Stockland. Are they alike in any way? Explain.

***Outline***

I. Thesis Statement: *Vivian Baxter Johnson and Dolores Stockland are more different than alike. They are alike in that both were probably once in love with Bailey, Sr., and that both live in California. They were different in that one is very inhibited and the other is not; one is older than the other; one is honest about who she is; one is hostile to Marguerite.*

II. Differences

A. Dolores younger than Vivian

B. Dolores not married to Bailey, Sr.

C. Dolores pretending to be what she is not

D. Dolores's mouth taut

E. Dolores hostile toward Marguerite

III. Similarities

A. Both probably once attracted by Bailey, Sr.

B. Both in California

***Topic #3***

Were there any long-range effects of the attack on Marguerite by Mr. Freeman? Explain your answer.

***Outline***

I. Thesis Statement: *There were several long-range effects of the rape on Marguerite, including her muteness, having her childhood taken away, her embarrassment, her injury, and her fear of Bailey's sexual experiments.*

II. Muteness

  A. Refused to talk, except to Bailey, Jr

  B. Did not talk for several years

III. Childhood taken away

  A. Felt old

  B. Did not feel young and carefree

IV. Embarrassment

  A. Wondered if others knew

  B. Felt embarrassed when disrobed in front of others

V. Injury

  A. Physical injuries which took weeks to heal

  B. Emotional injuries which took years to heal

  C. Still remembers well

VI. Fear of sex

  A. Feared for Bailey when he had sex with Joyce

  B. Feared that others would know of her rape

***Topic #4***

Marguerite tells her own story. Do you think an objective narrator could have presented the story better than someone who was so close to the story? Explain your answer.

***Outline***

I. Thesis Statement: *Marguerite tells her story more accurately and with more emotion and feeling than an objective narrator might. She is familiar with the time frame, the settings, the characters, and her own feelings and emotions.*

II. Time frame

   A. Has lived through the events

   B. Can understand time because was present

III. Settings

   A. Actually lived in South

   B. Actually lived in St. Louis and California

   C. Understood caste system of South

   D. Actually experienced the segregation, racism, and discrimination of St. Louis, California, and Stamps

IV. Characters

   A. Knew the characters

   B. Could depict their dialect

   C. Could describe accurately

V. Feelings and emotions

   A. Portrayed honestly—even the ugly emotions

   B. Remembered feelings

   C. Could describe since had felt

**SECTION FOUR**

# *Bibliography*

"A Wake-up Call from a Poet," *U.S. News and World Report,* February 1, 1993, p. 6–7.

Gillespie, Marcia Ann, "Maya Angelou in Living," *Essence,* December 1992, pp. 49–52, 120.

Lambert, Walter J. and Charles E. Lamb, *Reading Instruction in the Content Areas.* Chicago: Rand McNally Publishing Company, 1980.

Moritz, Charles (editor). *Current Biography Yearbook.* New York: H.W. Wilson Company, 1974.

"The Essence Award Winners," *Essence,* May 1992, p. 68.

*Introducing...*

# MAXnotes

## REA's Literature Study Guides

**MAXnotes**™ offer a fresh look at masterpieces of literature, presented in a live and interesting fashion. **MAXnotes**™ offer the essentials of what you should kno about the work, including outlines, explanations and discussions of the plo character lists, analyses, and historical context. **MAXnotes**™ are designed to he you think independently about literary works by raising various issues and though provoking ideas and questions. Written by literary experts who currently teach th subject, **MAXnotes**™ enhance your understanding and enjoyment of the work.

Available **MAXnotes**™ include the following:

**Animal Farm**
**Beowulf**
**The Canterbury Tales**
**Death of a Salesman**
**Divine Comedy I-Inferno**
**Gone with the Wind**
**The Grapes of Wrath**
**Great Expectations**
**The Great Gatsby**
**Hamlet**
**Huckleberry Finn**
**I Know Why the Caged Bird Sings**
**The Iliad**
**Julius Caesar**
**King Lear**
**Les Misérables**
**Macbeth**
**Moby Dick**
**1984**
**Of Mice and Men**
**The Odyssey**
**Paradise Lost**
**Plato's Republic**
**A Raisin in the Sun**
**Romeo and Juliet**
**The Scarlet Letter**
**A Tale of Two Cities**
**To Kill a Mockingbird**

RESEARCH & EDUCATION ASSOCIATION
61 Ethel Road W. • Piscataway, New Jersey 08854
Phone: (908) 819-8880

**Please send me more information about MAXnotes™.**

Name ______________________________

Address ______________________________

City ____________________ State ______ Zip ____________

THE BEST TEST PREPARATION FOR THE
GRE
GRADUATE
RECORD
EXAMINATION
LITERATURE
IN ENGLISH
6 Full-Length Exams
Completely Up-to-Date
based on the current format of the GRE Literature in English Test
➤ The ONLY test preparation book with detailed explanations to every exam question
➤ Far more comprehensive than any other test preparation book
Specially designed to depict the most recent GRE exams accurately, in both the type of questions and the level of difficulty
REA
Research & Education Association
Available at your local bookstore or order directly from us by sending in coupon below.
RESEARCH & EDUCATION ASSOCIATION
61 Ethel Road W., Piscataway, New Jersey 08854
Phone: (908) 819-8880
VISA
MasterCard
Charge Card Number
☐ Payment enclosed
☐ Visa ☐ Master Card
Expiration Date: ______ / ______
Mo Yr
Please ship "GRE Literature in English" @ $24.95 plus $4.00 for shipping.
Name
Address
City
State
Zip

*Available at your local bookstore or order directly from us by sending in coupon below.*

RESEARCH & EDUCATION ASSOCIATION
61 Ethel Road W., Piscataway, New Jersey 08854
Phone: (908) 819-8880

VISA MasterCard

☐ Payment enclosed
☐ Visa ☐ Master Card

Charge Card Number

Expiration Date: ______ / ______
Mo Yr

Please ship **"Handbook of English"** @ $15.95 plus $4.00 for shipping.

Name ____________________

Address ____________________

City ____________ State ______ Zip ______